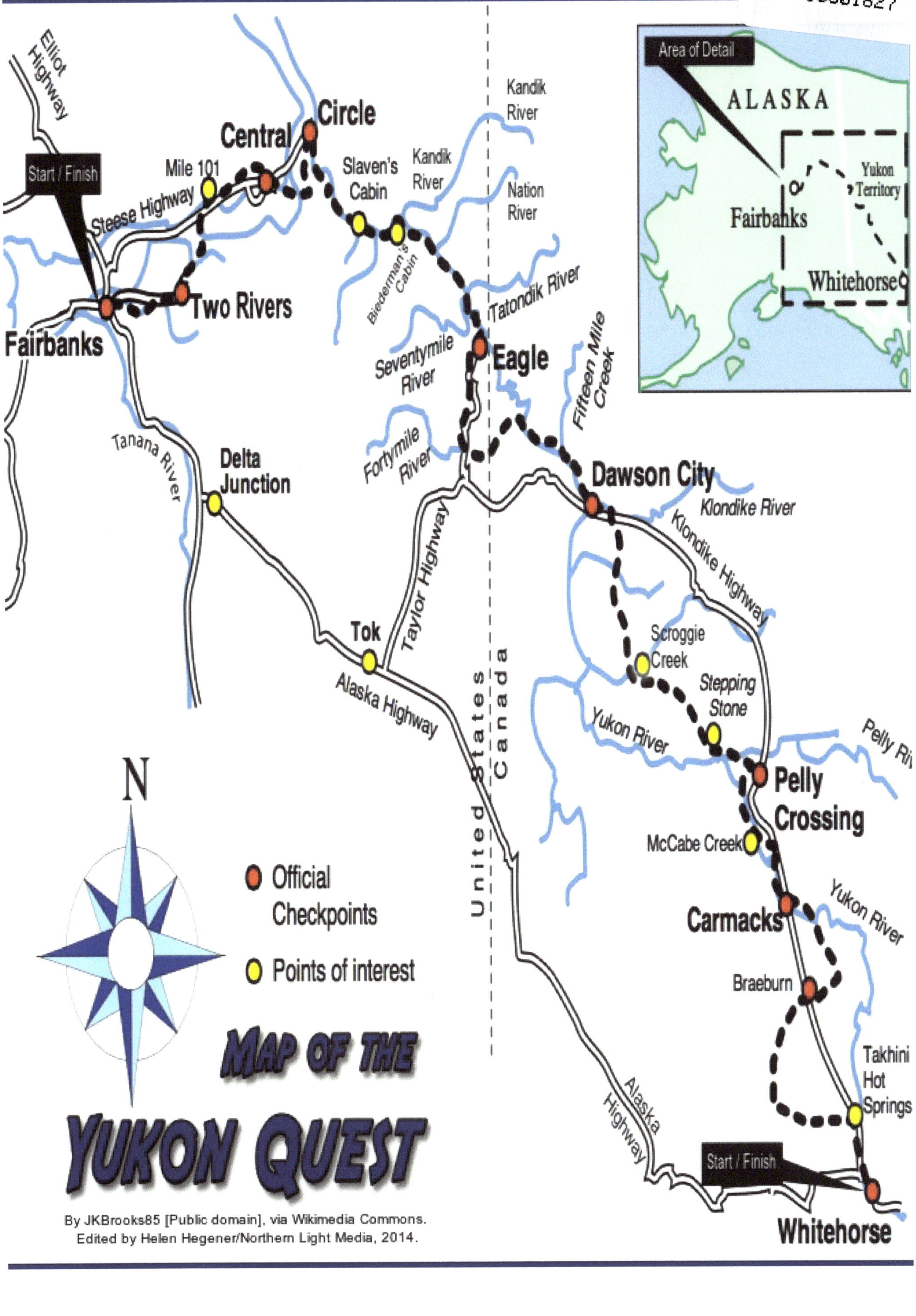

By JKBrooks85 [Public domain], via Wikimedia Commons.
Edited by Helen Hegener/Northern Light Media, 2014.

The Yukon Quest Trail

1,000 Miles Across Northern Alaska and the Yukon Territory

by Helen Hegener

Photographs by Helen Hegener, Eric Vercammen, and Scott Chesney

NORTHERN LIGHT MEDIA

*Left: Dyan Bergen's lead dog, 2013 Yukon Quest finish. [Eric Vercammen/Northern Light Media.
Above: Yukon Quest trail marker near Two Rivers. [Eric Vercammen/Northern Light Media]*

The Yukon Quest Trail

1,000 Miles Across Northern Alaska and the Yukon Territory

by Helen Hegener

Photographs by Helen Hegener, Eric Vercammen, and Scott Chesney

© 2014 by Helen Hegener, Northern Light Media. All rights reserved.
Photographs by Scott Chesney are ©Scott Chesney/Talespin Media. All rights reserved.

No part of this book may be reproduced or transmitted in any form or by any means, electronic or mechanical, including photocopying, recording, or by any information storage and retrieval system, in whole or in part, without written permission from the author and publisher, except for the inclusion of brief quotations for the purposes of reviewing this book.

First printing 2014 by Northern Light Media.
Printed in the United States of America.

ISBN-13: 978-0692340431 (Northern Light Media)
ISBN-10: 0692340432 (Northern Light Media)

1. Alaska. Yukon Territory, Canada. 2. Alaska, Yukon ~ Pictorial works.
Includes maps, bibliography, race archives, index.

Additional copies available
for $34.00 postpaid from:
Northern Light Media
Post Office Box 298023
Wasilla, Alaska 99629
http://northernlightmedia.wordpress.com

Cover Photo: Denis Tremblay near Central, 2013 Yukon Quest [by Eric Vercammen/Northern Light Media]
Above: Mike Ellis' all-Siberian team at the 2014 start in Fairbanks. [Helen Hegener/Northern Light Media]
Right: Torsten Kohnert, 2014 race, ready to drive his team 1,000 miles. [Helen Hegener/Northern Light Media]

Dedication

To all the people ~ and the dogs ~ who make this great race possible.

Have you broken trail on snowshoes,

mushed your huskies up the river,

dared the unknown, led the way,

and clutched the prize?

~ ~ ~ ~ ~

Robert Service

Above: Jodi Bailey finishing the 2011 Yukon Quest. [Helen Hegener/Northern Light Media]

Acknowledgements

There are literally hundreds of people to whom I owe a debt of gratitude for helping me come to the understanding which has produced this book. From the first trip to Dawson City with my daughter Jody, when I knew the name but not the incredible stories behind the Yukon Quest, I've dreamed of writing a book which might capture the history, the legacy, and the magic of this race. Jody first shared my excitement of discovering the magnificent land this race traverses, and when I travel it now I often think of her wonderment and awe at the beauty of the North.

Since then I've traveled the Yukon Quest trail with many friends, including Donna Quante, Jan DeNapoli Cosmutto, Jodi Bailey, Bonnie Foster, Albert Marquez, Nancy Steuer, Marlys Sauer, and all of the friendly familiar faces who make up the traveling roadshow which is the Yukon Quest each year: the volunteers, handlers, judges, vets, media, families and, of course, the mushers. Each of these people contributed, in large and small ways, to the knowledge and understanding I brought to this project.

There are two people who deserve special mention, however, because this book is graced by their beautiful photographs. One is my friend Scott Chesney, who answered my last-minute plea for photos of the Whitehorse end of the race, because, upon reviewing the final draft of the book, I was unhappy with my scant coverage of that half of the race. Scott graciously offered me hundreds of photos to select from, and this book is much richer and far more comprehensive for his gracious gesture.

Most of the photographs on the Alaskan side are the work of my dear friend Eric Vercammen, of Antwerp, Belgium, who travels to Alaska to photograph the sled dog races each season. In 2013, after years of listening to me describe the wonders of the Yukon Quest, he set out with me and our friend Albert Marquez to travel the Alaskan side of the race. Eric's images provide invaluable depth and perspective, and incredible beauty, to this book. Someday we'll travel the rest of the trail . . . .

Above: Brian Wilmshurst near Two Rivers, 2013 Yukon Quest. [Eric Vercammen/Northern Light Media]

DEDICATION	6
ACKNOWLEDGEMENTS	7
PREFACE	10
INTRODUCTION	12
MAP OF THE YUKON QUEST ROUTE	14
JOHN SCHANDELMEIER'S TRAIL NOTES	15
CHAPTER ONE: A BRIEF HISTORY OF THE YUKON QUEST	26
Named for the Historical Highway of the North	27
Rudiments and Purposes of the Race	28
The Morning of the First Yukon Quest	28
First Race Results	33
End of the Inaugural Running	35
CHAPTER TWO: FAIRBANKS	36
Meet the Mushers	38
Color and Spectacle Mark the Start	44
Odd-numbered Years Finish Here	46
Log Cabin Yukon Quest Office	50
CHAPTER THREE: TWO RIVERS	52
Nordale Bridge to the Pleasant Valley Store	54
Chena Hot Springs Road	58
Two Rivers Checkpoint	62
CHAPTER FOUR: MILE 101	66
At the Bottom of Eagle Summit	67
A Perilous Part of the Mail Route	68
Airlifted Off Eagle Summit	69
Crossing Eagle Summit	74
CHAPTER FIVE: CENTRAL	78
Mushing Down Main Street	79
Scenes from a Checkpoint	80
Arctic Circle Hot Springs	86

CHAPTER SIX: CIRCLE CITY 90
   The Checkpoint at the End of the Road 90
   On the Banks of the Yukon River 92
   At the Circle City Checkpoint 94

CHAPTER SEVEN: EAGLE 100
   The Remotest Checkpoint 101
   Slaven's, Biederman's, and Trout Creek 102
   80 Sled Dogs and A Legendary Mail Carrier 104
   The Handlers' Trail: A Long Drive 106

CHAPTER EIGHT: DAWSON CITY 108
   A Mandatory Layover 109
   Dawson City Checkpoint 110
   Veterinary Care 116
   Gold Rush City 118
   Mushers 121

CHAPTER NINE: PELLY CROSSING 124
   Home of the Selkirk First Nation 125
   Pelly Crossing Checkpoint 126

CHAPTER TEN: CARMACKS 128
   Named for George Washington Carmack 128
   Scenes at the Carmacks Checkpoint 130

CHAPTER ELEVEN: BRAEBURN 132
   World's Largest Cinnamon Buns 133
   Takhini River 135

CHAPTER TWELVE: WHITEHORSE 136
   The Alternate Start and Finish Line 136
   Downtown Whitehorse 138
   The 2013 Start 140

MAP, BOOKS, CHAMPIONS, INDEX 144

Above: Author Helen Hegener on the Yukon Quest trail, at Eagle Summit during the 2014 race. [Photo by Bonnie Foster]
Below: License plate on Hugh Neff's dogtruck. Neff won the Yukon Quest in 2012. [Helen Hegener/Northern Light Media]

Preface

My first exposure to the Yukon Quest was in Dawson City, Yukon Territory, in 2008, as Lance Mackey was coming up the Yukon River and into the Dawson City checkpoint beside the great riverboat, Keno. My business partner at the time, Donna Quante, had driven us over 1,000 miles just in time to see Lance's team coming up the trail. We took a quick look around and determined the two best places to shoot video footage, down on the river and up at the checkpoint on Main Street, and we split up to capture both positions. I got the checkpoint, and it was a thrill to get a close look at Lance's team, strong hardy dogs decked out in red coats who'd just brought him all the way from the distant Fairbanks start.

I listened to Lance's handlers call each dog by name: Rev, Dred, Zorro, Boycuz, Hansome, Larry... I would become familiar with each dog in the weeks ahead as we followed Lance through two more major long distance races, the Iditarod and the All Alaska Sweepstakes, and the video we shot would become our documentary DVD, *Appetite and Attitude: A Conversation with Lance Mackey* [Northern Light Media, 2008].

I fell in love with the Yukon Quest on that first trip. I was already familiar with the country, having traveled through Alaska and the Yukon for over 30 years. I'd even been to Dawson City before, but this was different, the entire town was absorbed in the race, and it was a heady experience.

Above: Lance Mackey coming up the Yukon River and into Dawson City on his way to winning his fourth consecutive Yukon Quest in 2008. *Below:* Trail note at the Circle City checkpoint, 2011. [Helen Hegener/Northern Light Media]

Since that time I've been to almost every mid- and long-distance sled dog race in Alaska, I've helped create two races and have volunteered for several, and the Yukon Quest remains my hands-down favorite. Crossing great mountain ranges, traveling the loneliest stretches of the mighty Yukon River, with checkpoints spaced minimally and the weather conditions often extreme, this race challenges mushers like no other, and it always challenges me to capture the intensity, the excitement, and the drama of each year's running.

Since that first Yukon Quest in 2008 I have not missed a race. I've been at the start and the finish in Fairbanks on alternate years, always a wonderful opportunity to spend time with friends. I've attended the awards ceremonies, waited alongside the trail for teams to materialize out of the brush, and I've slept beside the Yukon River with the northern lights dancing wildly overhead. I've been one of the lucky few who has had the opportunity to travel to the distant checkpoints of this epic race, often in the company of good friends and media colleagues, and I've tried to share that adventure with others through my writing, my photographs, and my videos. This book is another attempt to share my love of this great sport, and this epic race, with others.

Helen Hegener
Meadow Lakes, Alaska

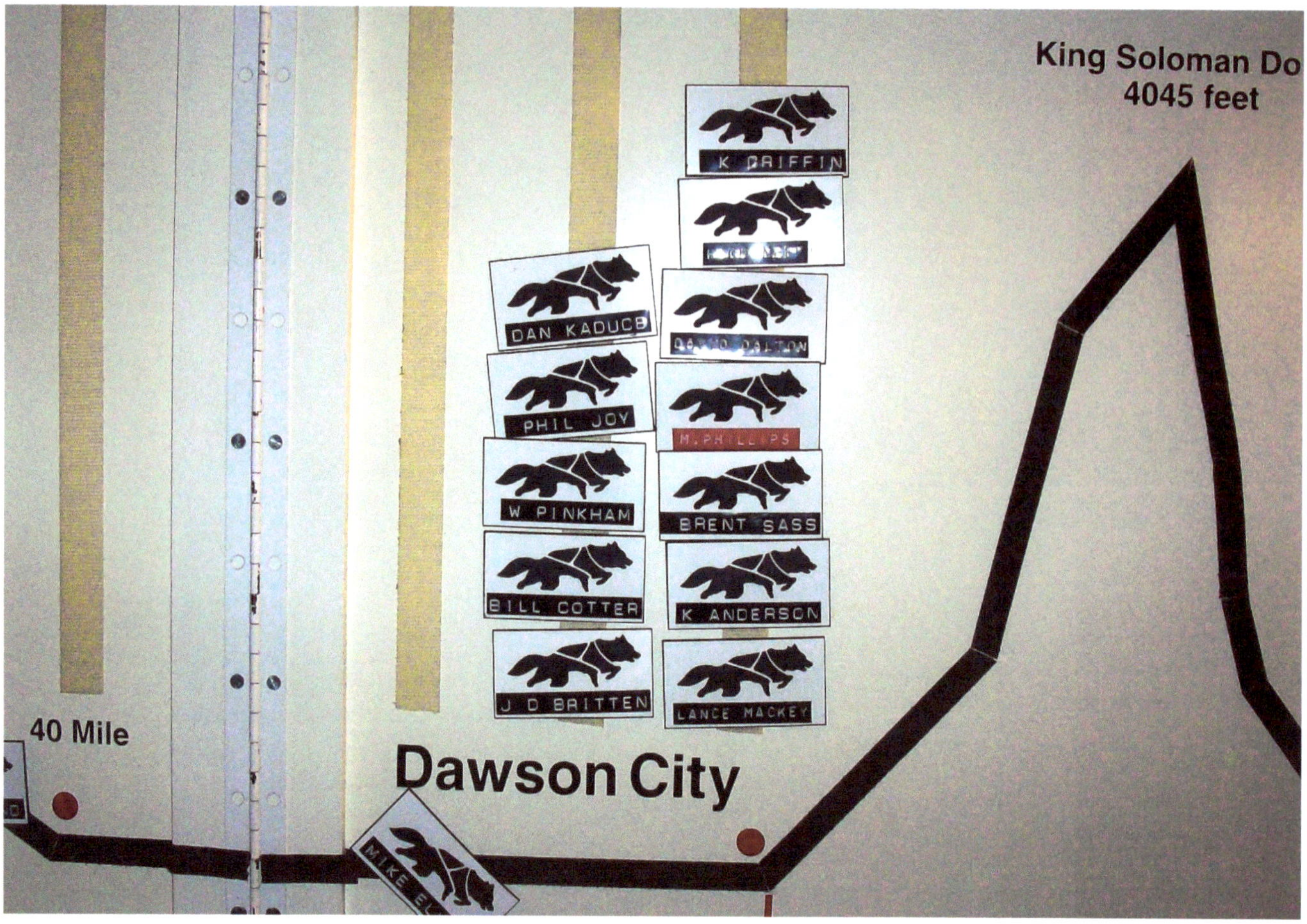

Introduction

The Toughest Sled Dog Race in the World

The Yukon Quest trail is close enough to one thousand miles long that no one disputes its claim to being one of only two 1,000 mile sled dog races in the world – the other being the more widely-known Iditarod Trail Sled Dog Race from Anchorage to Nome. The distances are similar, but that is where the similarities end, for the Yukon Quest has far fewer checkpoints, crosses many more mountains, and the temperatures are more often extreme, sometimes even necessitating a change in the race route.

In his book *Yukon Quest, The Story of the World's Toughest Sled Dog Race*, Lew Freedman wrote, "Some believe the Quest is the toughest race on the face of the earth. In truth, in any given year, the weather dictates whether that is a reality."

Braeburn, Carmacks, Pelly Crossing . . .

This book is organized into chapters which correlate to the Yukon Quest checkpoints, beginning in Fairbanks and traveling east to Whitehorse. There are fewer than ten; the Iditarod has more than twice as many checkpoints along the same distance. There are four checkpoints more than 100 miles apart, and there are over 200 miles between Pelly Crossing and Dawson City, with only a dog drop between them.

The Yukon Quest trail climbs over four summits: Rosebud, Eagle, American, and King Solomon's Dome; and it travels the upper reaches of the Yukon River, about which journalist John Balzar wrote in *Yukon Alone*, "...the ice rises, great broken walls of it, a jumbled labyrinth continuing for miles. Just as unsettling are the periodic open leads we see on the Yukon. Some are just cracks; others are geometric rectangles a hundred feel long where the ice has vanished and the wind froths wavelets on pure blue water."

A Living Memorial

The Yukon Quest website explains that the race "was founded on the premise that a dog driver and his team should be a self-sufficient unit; capable of challenging varied terrain and severe weather conditions. The race is a living memorial to those turn-of-the-century miners, trappers, and mail carriers who opened up the country without benefit of snowmobiles, airplanes, or roads. It was their strength and fortitude that blazed the Trail over which most of the Yukon Quest travels."

There is a palpable sense of history inherent in this great race, for the mushers and their teams literally run in the tracks of some of the greatest sled dog drivers of all time.

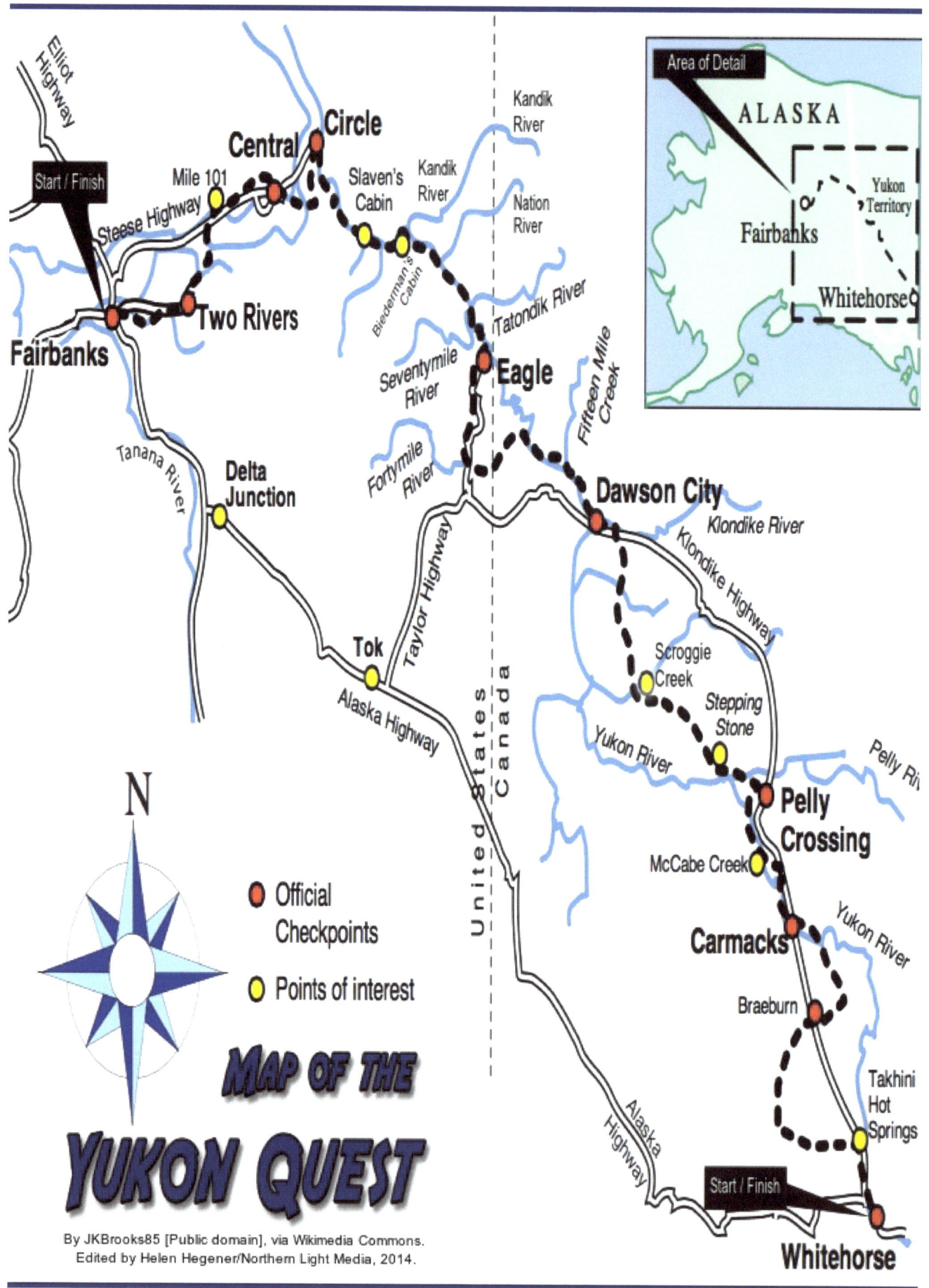

The Yukon Quest Trail

John Schandelmeier's Trail Notes

The Yukon Quest trail follows old gold mining and mail delivery routes across mountains, over lakes, and along the rivers of northeastern Alaska and the Yukon Territory of Canada. The trail travels some of the harshest country in the world at the worst time of the year, when the land truly is, as Robert Service described it, "locked tight as a drum."

Across frozen lakes and rivers, down creeks harboring dangerous overflow, over mountain passes which demand the teams almost defy gravity to cross them . . . . The Yukon Quest trail demands the highest caliber of skill and readiness from mushers and their teams. Many who start don't make it to the finish. Those mushers who do finish have accomplished something to be proud of, a challenge daunting enough that few mushers ever even attempt it: The World's Toughest Sled Dog Race.

Two-time Yukon Quest Champion John Schandelmeier compiled a descriptive guide to the trail, and has generously given permission to share it here. Besides winning the 1992 and 1996 Yukon Quest Championships, John has finished the Yukon Quest twenty times, and has also won the 1997 Yukon Quest Sportsmanship Award, and the 1994 and 1996 Veterinarian's Choice Award for Excellence in Dog Care. John's Trail Notes, *Fairbanks to Whitehorse* first, followed by the *Whitehorse to Fairbanks* route.

Fairbanks to Whitehorse

Even Numbered Years The Race Starts in Fairbanks. The distances given are based on the 2009 trail; along some of the river trails, distances may vary slightly from year to year.

Fairbanks to Two Rivers checkpoint: (approx. 72 miles)

From the start line you will be traveling thru downtown Fairbanks and parts of Fort Wainwright on the Chena River. The river is well-traveled and there be more than one trail choice. Stay on the Chena. Houses will change to cabins and become sparse. You pass under the Nordale Road Bridge 17 miles out. 5 1/2 miles further you will leave the Chena R. on the left-hand side. The trail takes you around some fields and on to a well-used trail that runs predominately east. This is the Baseline Trail. You will have several road-crossings, (more like well-used driveways), along this trail. Approximately 10 - 15 miles along this you will begin to encounter more housing, and occasional dog yards—you are entering the Pleasant Valley area. A left turn 15 miles along the baseline will put you on the Pleasant Valley Rd. You will run this road to the Chena Hotsprings Road, turn right and parallel that road past Pleasant Valley Store, (did you forget anything?), a Laundromat and several other businesses. The store is just about 40 miles from the start line. You will be on a well-traveled trail for the next 35 miles. Three miles past the store you will cross the Chena Hotspring's Road. Expect overflow at creek crossings. You cross under the Hotsprings road 24 miles out, then again 28 miles out. 2 miles past Angel Creek Lodge is the Mile 52 Chena Hotsprings Rd. checkpoint.

Mile 52 Chena Hotsprings Road to Mile 101: (approx. 41 miles)

You are in an area with recreational cabins and numerous driveways for about 3 miles before turning more northerly up the N. Fork of the Chena River. Expect more overflow as you climb gradually up the trail that parallels the N.F. 17 miles out of the checkpoint you climb steeply up to Boulder Summit. Rosebud Ridge is usually rocky, you are on top, (above timber), for about 3 or 4 miles as you traverse Boulder then Rosebud Summits. Boulder Summit is well-named, Rosebud is not. Expect wind, poor visibility and poor braking conditions. A gradually 5 mile descent thru the trees lands you in the Birch Cr. drainage. The trail follows along the side of Birch Cr. crossing several small drainages—again---expect overflow. The trail gradually improves as you approach the 101 checkpoint. 7 miles from 101 you will come up to the side of the Steese Highway and parallel that road into the checkpoint. You are in a mining district so expect tailing piles, gravel and some glare ice. Parking at 101 can be tight; come prepared for windy conditions here. Snow cover may be minimal. You are 112 miles from town.

Mile 101 to Central: (approx. 28 miles)

Leaving 101 you will be traveling thru an active mining area; lots of gravel and glare ice for the first 3-4 mile. It's 6 miles to Eagle Summit; the last few miles will be windblown tundra, not overly steep from this side. There are 13 tripods in place to lead you up and over the ridge. You will be on top for less than ¼ mile before you begin a very steep descent, snow will be windblown with poor braking on this drop, A few hundred yards from the top on your descent will be a dogleg to the right. Don't miss this! Contour over a few hundred yards, slightly climbing to a bump on the ridgeline, from there the trail heads straight down to tree line. Expect lousy braking and rutted conditions. You will survive; usually the little worse for wear. The trail continues to wind down into Mammoth Cr., usually overflows. You will cross the Steese 13 miles from 101 and again be in and out of mining areas and a burn. 2 miles from Central you come up on the Steese and run along the road for a short distance, dive off the left-side to avoid a blind corner, than back on the road into the Central checkpoint. Good facilities and parking. You are 140 miles out.

Central to Circle City: (approx. 75 miles)

Leaving Central you will follow the Circle Hotsprings road for 8 miles. From the Hotsprings airstrip it's 11 miles across Medicine Lake and thru the swamps to Birch Cr. (Expect temperatures on Birch Cr. to be 15 degrees colder than Central). 30 miles on Birch Cr. you pass under the Steese Highway Bridge. Carl Cochrans place is just beyond the Bridge. This may or may not be open, parking tight. It's roughly 17 miles on Birch Cr. from the bridge to the exit on the north bank; 8 more miles to the Circle checkpoint. ¼ mile from the checkpoint you will come up on the road----follow it to the checkpoint. Parking is fair; facilities are good. It's almost always cold here. You are 215 miles from the start.

Circle City to Eagle, Alaska: (approx. 163-167 miles)

Immediately after leaving the Circle checkpoint you will be routed onto the Yukon. Conditions along this river vary considerably from one year to the next. The trail will cross the river a few times, you will possibly be off of the Yukon for short stretches, depending on ice conditions. Brian Asplund's cabin is at 21 mile, south bank at the mouth of a slough. It is rough but has a stove. Richard Smith's is 43 miles out of Circle, on the left bank of the Yukon. There is firewood and good parking. 17 miles beyond Smith's is Slaven's Roadhouse, excellent facilities for mushers; parking for dogs is only fair. You can pass this stop by staying on the river trail, with the bypass trail rejoining in approx ¼ mile. It is 23 miles from Slavens to the mouth of the Kandik and its cabin. You are a long 80 out of Circle. The next landmark of note will be across from the Nation River at the mouth of 4th of July Cr. (27 from Kandik) There will be a fish rack on the Yukon and a side trail leading off the Quest Trail up a slough 1 mile to the Henry's place. 9 miles further is Trout Creek (45 miles from Eagle) and Mike Sager's cabin. This is good stop with sheltered parking, though more than 6 teams is crowded. Trout Cr. is off of the main trail—there is a sign and the trail is a short loop thru. Above Trout Cr. there are a few portage possibilities. We usually take only one; that from the mouth of the 70-mile River skirting behind Calico Bluffs. Departing this portage you pass through Andy and Kate's homestead, you are 12 miles from town. As you approach Eagle, you will either see the town or the lights of town a couple miles out. The Eagle checkpoint has good parking for dogs and excellent facilities for mushers. You are 382 miles from Fairbanks and 152 miles from Dawson City, Yukon.

Eagle to Dawson City: (approx. 150 miles)

Leaving Eagle you will be on the Taylor Highway for a short 50 miles---there are mile posts; Eagle is Milepost 162. You have some potentially nasty glaciers along the road for the first 10 miles. About 20 miles of gradual climbing from Eagle will take you up on American Summit. Expect wind, some gravel, sidehill conditions and poor visibility. You will be above timber for about 4 miles. Mile 138 will have you back in the trees, under cover. Winding road, ups and downs until you reach the 40-Mile Bridge. Immediately after crossing the bridge you drop down onto the 40-Mile River. Expect it to be cold. Sometimes overflow, but a normally fast trail for the next 45 miles. Approximately halfway down the 40-mile to its confluence with the Yukon, you will cross into Canada. The 40-Mile is in a deep canyon for most of the way; expect little sun. Clinton Cr. is 41 miles from the Bridge and 4 miles above the confluence of the Yukon and the 40-Mile Rivers. Good hospitality. The old town of 40 Mile also is a great hospitality stop and has excellent cover for dogs. Just out of 40-Mile, you jump on the Yukon for the final 50-odd miles to Dawson. The trail crosses back and forth along the Yukon depending on ice conditions. There may be some short portages. Cor Guimond's cabin is 38 miles from Dawson and the 15-Mile River (recognizable because there is almost always overflow at the mouth), about 20 miles from Dawson. The checkpoint at Dawson is in the middle of town. After checking in, you will be directed to

the dog holding area which is about a half-mile away across the river. You are about 550 miles from Fairbanks and about 450 miles from the finish line.

Dawson City to Pelly Crossing: (205-210 miles)

Watch your markers leaving town; you are on the Yukon for a short distance, then up the Klondike R. for a mile or so, before crossing several parking lots and driveways before turning right into the Klondike mining district. You will travel a plowed road for some distance---varying from year to year; you will exit this road to the left; very well-marked, and enter a narrower mining road that is almost never plowed……easy road grade, but a steady climb to the top of King Solomon Dome---25 miles out. You will see a lighted communications tower on your left not far off of the trail; just past that, beginning the downgrade off the Dome, there is a 120 degree turn to your right; if you miss this turn you are sleeping---there are trees across trail and dozens of stakes---some may be down if you are not the first to reach there……. A long downgrade (with overflows) brings you to the Indian River bridge; mile 50. Cold spot. You are entering the Black Hills; some long winding climbs, overflow and there can be sporadic drifting as you climb. Climbs are road-grade, trail is good. As you summit---the drop toward the Stewart R. and the Scroggie Cr. dog drop is into another fairly active mining district. The notable landmark is a series of switchbacks coming out of the Black Hills. There are 13 if you are awake, 9-- if you are not. It is 25 miles from the bottom of the switchbacks to Scroggie Cr. overflow. 3 miles from the Dog drop you will be on the Stewart R. Climb the bank again and you are there. Marginal facilities, limited parking, cold. 105 miles from Dawson. 70 to the hospitality stop at Stepping Stone.

The trail from Scroggie to Stepping Stone is again on the mining roads. Overflow. Few recognizable landmarks, though Jane Cr. Summit is about half-way; you are not above timber, but the spruce are somewhat sparse…. A few miles prior to Stepping Stone, you go past Pelly Farms, (cows), and drop onto the Pelly River. Stepping Stone has excellent hospitality, cold water, good dog parking. 35 miles to Pelly. Normally you will be on the Pelly River all of the way to Pelly Crossing---some years you may have to jump onto the plowed road that leads to Pelly Farm if the River conditions are poor. You go under the bridge to the checkpoint at Pelly; the checkpoint has been in various places over the years, but the hospitality and parking have always been very good. You are 770 miles from Fairbanks and about 240 from Whitehorse.

Pelly Crossing to Carmacks: (75-80 miles)

You will leave Pelly on a plowed road that quickly turns unmaintained and then into trails. Varying conditions of mostly flat running, (2 lakes about half-way), will take you 25 miles to the Klondike Highway still some 7 miles from the dogdrop at McCabe Cr. You follow the highway to McCabe Cr. and normally cross under the bridge before getting on a short plowed road to the stop at McCabe. Hospitality is excellent, parking for dogs is fair. There is water available. You are 32 miles from Pelly---44 or so to Carmacks. Cross the Yukon out of McCabe; you will get into a recent burn, the trail is on and off of the Yukon; ice may be rough. Much of this trail will be firebreaks; straight and unremarkable. Snow cover may be light on some of the grades. 15 miles from Carmacks you will come onto the Freegold Road. It is seldom plowed and excellent running the rest of the way in. As you approach Carmacks you will reach a hilly section; short grades. You will reach Pelly and travel thru town for a short mile to the Checkpoint. Parking is somewhat exposed, facilities are good for mushers. You are about 845 miles from Fairbanks and 170-odd from the finish.

Carmacks to Braeburn: (70-75 miles)

You leave Carmacks on the Yukon---under the Bridge then onto bush trails. There are some challenging short hills; you will be on and off of the Yukon R. 25-28 miles out you are on Mandana Lake; this is the beginning of the Chain of Lakes. These lakes have numerous portages and some overflow; they provide some great trail and some very good resting spots. 17 miles from Braeburn you reach Cogland Lake; you are on this Lake for 7 miles, once off; you climb a steep bank---it is 10 miles to Braeburn. Cross the Klondike Highway and you are at the checkpoint. It is 100 miles to the finish. Parking is good, facilities for mushers are excellent.

Braeburn to the Finish: (100 miles)

From Braeburn to town, the trail is mixed timber with a few lakes, (early), creek crossings, etc. Excellent trail, sometimes low snow. 70 miles along you reach the Tahkini River. You are 30 miles from town---18 miles of twisting river takes you, [under the Klondike Highway bridge], to the confluence of the Tahkini and the final 12 mile run on the Yukon to the Finish. 1,015 miles; give or take.

• • • •

Alternate Yukon River run to Eagle.

If the trail up and over American Summit is impassable, the alternate Quest route is the Yukon River. The trail is the same as far as the 40-mile hospitality stop. From that point, instead of turning up the 40-mile River, teams will say on the Yukon River. The Yukon provides a flat and relatively fast 50 miles to Eagle. There are a few bush trails that are used to cut off bends and avoid jumble ice. Snow conditions are usually good, though it can be windblown around the US/Canadian border. The border will not be visible at night, and is tough to spot at any time. The Border crossing is fourteen miles from Eagle by River, but the trail will take you off of the Yukon and into the woods for six-eight miles prior to reaching the Eagle checkpoint. You will follow road edges and power lines before coming into the back of the checkpoint at the old school house.

Whitehorse to Fairbanks

Odd Numbered Years The Race Starts in Whitehorse. Mileages and times given are based on dog team speeds. They are estimates; we trust you will find them reasonably accurate. The Trail may vary slightly from year to year.

Whitehorse to Braeburn: (Long 100 miles)

You will be on the Yukon River for the first 12 miles of trail, then up the Takhini for approx. 18 miles. You climb the right-hand bank to intersect with the Old Dawson Overland Trail. You will be on this trail for about 70 miles. Good timber on a relatively easy section of trail. There are a couple of hills that can be challenging on the downhill. There are plenty of places to take a break; not many recognizable landmarks for the rookie. If you have questions; talk to Frank Turner. 5 miles from the Braeburn checkpoint you will encounter a very steep, short downhill on to Braeburn Lake. Cross the Lake and back onto the trail with a left turn.

The Braeburn checkpoint has good services and fair conditions for parking. It will be crowded.

Braeburn to Carmacks: (approx. 70 miles)

This section of trail can be one of the most challenging on the entire race. You will be on narrow trails, creeks with overflow; some of it potentially deep. Low snow can make this section tough on sleds. Immediately upon leaving Braeburn, you cross the Klondike Highway; it is about 18 miles, give or take, to Cogland Lake. You will turn left onto Cogland and stay on the Lake for 7 miles. For the next 30 miles you will be on and off of various small lakes and ponds. There are many good camping spots with fair firewood. There is a good open creek about halfway to Carmacks where you can get water. A good landmark is Mandana Lake which is about 28 miles from the Carmacks Checkpoint. You will stay on this Lake for almost 5 miles. The remainder of the trail to Carmacks is mostly narrow, heavily timbered with some steep hills. You will go down onto the Yukon River for several short sections and see your first jumble ice. Go under the Yukon River bridge and climb the left-hand bank; the checkpoint is within ¼ mile. The Checkpoint at Carmacks has been in several different locations over the years, so follow the markers………

Carmacks has good Checkpoint facilities but is not a great place for resting dogs. The holding area is usually plowed and teams will be parked closely. Yukon Quest and YQ300 teams will still be close at this point; if that is the case, you may consider camping elsewhere so your dogs get a good rest.

Carmacks to Pelly Crossing: (approx. 75-80 miles)

Follow markers closely out of this checkpoint; you are traveling thru town for a mile or so before turning right onto the Freegold road. You stay on this road for approximately 15 miles; it is usually very good, at times in the past it has been plowed, but always has had a good snow base. You will leave the road onto a firebreak trail---straight ahead off the right side of the road in a corner; almost impossible to miss. You will be on this type of trail; firebreaks and cat trails until just before you reach the Dog Drop at McCabe Creek. You will be on and off of the Yukon. There are some sections of burn the closer you get to McCabe. Immediately prior to reaching McCabe; come down from a burned area and cross the Yukon, McCabe is up the far bank. McCabe has good parking for teams, fair facilities for drivers. Usually has hot water.

You leave McCabe up the driveway, cross the Klondike Highway under the Bridge or over the road, depending on how high the creek has overflowed. It is 32 miles to Pelly. You will follow the power line side parallel to the highway for 5, (endless) miles---almost always punchy and slow, before turning right up a relay site access road and on to the very good, fast trail to Pelly. Watch for a short steep section down on to a creek just after you leave the road. You will be in a burn area first, with several short hills and a couple of overflowed creeks. The trail flattens and crosses several lakes just farther than half-way to the Pelly checkpoint. You will see the lights of town at the top of a pretty good downgrade; you are less than 5 miles out. The Pelly Checkpoint has been in various places over the year; always the parking and hospitality are very good.

Pelly Crossing to Dawson City: (approx. 205-210 miles)

You will leave Pelly on to the river and under the bridge. At times, if the river has bad ice conditions, you may jump up onto a plowed road for a couple of miles---or 20—depending…… Usually you will stay on the Pelly River all of the way to Stepping Stone. The trail is usually fast down the River. A few miles prior to Stepping Stone you will pass Pelly Farms. Cows. More often than not the trail is on the opposite side of the Yukon River from the farm.

Stepping Stone is a hospitality stop approximately 35 miles from Pelly Crossing. They have cold water and sleeping facilities; there is good parking. From Stepping Stone the trail crosses the River, runs by the farm and up a fairly long grade to get you out of the Pelly valley. It is 70 miles to the Dog Drop at Scroggie Creek on the Stewart River. The trail is thru good timber, up and down, with many small overflowed creeks. One recognizable landmark is Jane Creek Summit on the long side of halfway; it is not above timber, but it does get you up at the brush line. 11 miles prior to the Scroggie Creek Dog Drop, you will begin to parallel Scroggie Creek The parking facilities at Scroggie can get crowded in a hurry, plus it is the coldest spot between Pelly and Dawson. As a rule; facilities for mushers are marginal to poor.

Leaving Scroggie, you drop onto the Stewart River, cross and head upriver about 5 miles and into the timber; you will be in fair trees for 5-7 miles before entering a mining district with little cover. Good place to break in the timber and a bit warmer as you climb. The mining district has overflows that will be wet. 25 miles from the Stewart you will climb a series of switchbacks into the Blackhills. Anywhere from 9-13 switchbacks--- depending on how tired you are……You will be in the Blackhills for 20 miles; up and down, overflow in spots but basically good trail on a road grade which continues all the way to the Klondike Highway just outside of Dawson.

Indian River bridge is approximately 55 miles from Scroggie and 50 from Dawson. Not much timber there and cold as it is in the valley. Shortly after the bridge you will come to the Granville forks and you will turn left to travel up Sulphur Creek. After about 10 miles you will start your climb to the top of King Solomon Dome from here. It is a gradual climb; expect some overflows. There is a communications tower on top that, in good weather, can be seen for miles away. Be sure you turn sharply left at the intersection near the tower; it is always very well marked, but almost every year someone takes the wrong turn. You will still climb after the turn, but soon pass below just the tower and you will be on the 25 mile downgrade into Dawson. Again, this is road-grade; it will be plowed the last few miles into town. You will make a left turn near the Klondike Highway near town and cross a couple of parking lots before dropping onto the river trail for the last couple of miles to the checkpoint. Follow the markers closely; they are usually very good. The Checkpoint is off the River (on your right) on the main street. Once checked in, your handler will direct you to the holding area which is a half mile away.

Dawson City to Eagle: (approx. 150 miles)

The first 50 miles of your way from Dawson are on the Yukon River; the first 20 miles are usually fairly fast and smooth—likely to be overflow at the mouth of the 15 Mile drainage, (It is recognizable as the only large drainage coming in on the N.E. side, Right-hand) The trail crosses back and forth across the Yukon and may use several bush trails for short distances, depending on ice conditions. The 40-mile hospitality stop is a long 50 miles most years. This is a good place to stop; adequate parking.

Leaving the old town of 40 Mile; you turn immediately left up the 40 Mile river. A few miles farther on is another hospitality stop at Clinton Creek—just up the 40 Mile River past the bridge. You will be on the 40-Mile for 45 miles. It is a narrow, winding river that is most often cold because of the deep canyon with little sun. The trail usually is very good unless there has been a recent heavy snow—then expect overflow. You will be leaving the 40 Mile River at the Taylor Highway crossing. You climb up the boat ramp on the left bank, turn right on the Taylor Highway. You are at milepost 113 on the Taylor Highway. Crossing the bridge it is 49 miles to the checkpoint of Eagle at milepost 162. Highway running on good trail, with lots of ups and downs for this section.

Your first potentially windy summit of the trail is American Summit; if it's breezy in the trees below the summit expect possible whiteout conditions on top. You begin your climb just past milepost 135 and will get above timber a few miles further on. The summit is almost always side-hilled badly, markers can be frosted over, even in the wind. Expect hard, drifted snow. You are on top for about 3 miles before beginning your 20 mile descent to Eagle. The long gradual descent is mostly uneventful; you will encounter some potentially nasty overflow stretches as you near the town of Eagle; the worst of them between 4-8 miles out. The Checkpoint (M.P. 162) is the old schoolhouse on your right hand as you come toward the center of town. Well marked. Good parking for dogs, good facilities for mushers.

Eagle to Circle City: (approx. 162 miles)

The Yukon River ice can be rough. Prior to race start check on the ice conditions so you will be prepared. The Yukon is mostly flat running though there may be some side slopes depending on river levels at freeze-up. Prevailing winds come down the Yukon River. You will be on the river the entire way to Circle with the exception of a few short portages. Whether the trail uses the portages or no,

depends on ice conditions at freeze-up. Andy and Kate's homestead at mile 12 is your first landmark, Tatonduk River (Sheep Creek) comes in from the right at 28 mile, 43 miles downriver from Eagle you will reach a hospitality stop at Trout Creek (Mike Sager cabin). It is on a short cut-off left from the main trail—there will be a sign. Good warm-up spot, parking for more than 6 teams will be tight.

Leaving Trout Creek you will head north down the Yukon River. Below the mouth of the Nation, expect an icy trail with minimal snow for 5-6 miles; in the event of downed markers/windy conditions with poor visibility; generally stay toward the North bank. The trail returns to snow along this bank near the end of this section. Near Washington Cr. is another usually windblown and icy section of trail. Trout Creek to the mouth of the Kandik River is 37 miles, approx 80 miles from Eagle, there is a warm-up cabin here; good firewood available, easy to heat. 18 – 20 miles from the Kandik mouth is Slaven's Roadhouse. Good facilities for mushers, fair spot for dogs. You are 100 miles from Eagle and it is less then 60 miles to Circle.

From here it is 17 miles to Richard Smith's cabin—on the north bank, and about 19 more to Doug Dill's cabin. (South bank in the mouth of a slough. This cabin is rough since the 09 flood) Both cabins will be marked. It's about 21 miles to Circle from Dill's; count on rough ice for the last half of this trail into Circle. You will see the light from the airport beacon prior to reaching town. The checkpoint is on the main street in the middle of town. There is fair parking for dogs, good facilities for mushers Expect it to be cold.

Circle City to Central: (approx. 75 miles)

Leaving Circle you are on the road for ¼ mile, then off on a trap line trail, (right side), for 8 miles to Birch Creek. Expect it to be 15 degrees colder on Birch Creek than in Circle. 15 miles of Birch Creek will bring you to Carl Cochran's place which may or may not be open. Just out from Carl's you cross under the highway bridge, (Steese Highway); it is a short 50 miles to Central, with 30 plus miles on Birch Creek. It is winding, endless, and almost always the coldest section of the Yukon Quest. Be prepared for minus 60. Expect overflow and beautiful Northern Lights…

Birch Creek will noticeably narrow and soon you leave the creek on the southwest bank for a 11 mile run to the Circle Hot Springs road; much of this run is through exposed swamps. Medicine Lake is just past half-way. You cross the Hot Springs airstrip and parallel the road for 8 miles on the power line to the Central checkpoint. Good parking for dogs, good facilities for mushers.

Central to Mile 101: (approx. 28 miles)

You leave Central on the highway, make a small detour off the left side a mile out to avoid a blind corner, cross the road and run a 14 mile section thru swamps, firebreaks and mining areas. At the base of Eagle Summit you will cross the Steese Highway and again be in a mining district while gradually climbing 9 miles toward the summit. There is an important dogleg in this climb; ½ mile below the top you will come to the first of 13 large tripods which mark the route. You will angle right, keeping the higher slopes of the mountain on your left and slightly drop before turning sharply back left and climbing the last ¼ mile on the steepest section of the trail. This is almost always very hard windblown snow. Remove booties for traction, some mushers carry ice cleats for their boots for here. The top of Eagle Summit is less than ¼ mile wide, windblown with tundra showing.

Braking down the 101 side is fair, however, and it is not as steep. 6 miles to checkpoint Mile 101, straight down the valley. Watch for windblown ice, overflow, and bare gravel. There are fair facilities here for dogs and mushers. You are just shy of 39 miles to Chena Hotsprings Rd., a bit over 41 to the next checkpoint.

Mile 101 to 52 Chena Hotsprings Rd: (approx. 41 miles)

Leaving 101 you will follow along the road for 7 miles, in and out of the ditch or on a parallel trail depending on overflow. Near 94 mile of the Steese, you leave the edge of the road and drop into the Birch Creek headwaters. There will be a few overflowed creeks over the next few miles as you travel up the valley on your way to Rosebud Summit. You cross Birch Creek one last time and begin the long ascent toward Rosebud; it is a 5 mile steady climb.

Once near the top, Rosebud Summit consists of a series of short climbs and descents, it usually is pretty good traveling, with fair braking on the down hills. The last descent drops you into the timber at the head of the N. Fork of the Chena River. A very steep descent through burned timber; watch for tree roots that catch your brake; avoid trees when possible…….. It's about 14 miles to Chena Hotsprings Rd. from the pass, another 3 to the checkpoint at mile 52 of the Hot Springs Rd. You will have an 8-hour mandatory layover here. Use it wisely and remember that you are around 70 miles from the finish line.

Two Rivers Checkpoint to Fairbanks: (approx. 72 miles)

Watch for recreational teams, snowmachines and skiers from here to town. 2 miles out from the checkpoint you pass Angel Creek. The trail crosses under the Chena Hot Springs road two times---the first crossing is 28 miles from Pleasant Valley, the second 24 miles. This section of trail is well-traveled and relatively fast; expect overflow at the creeks as everywhere.

2 miles before Pleasant Valley Store you will cross over the Chena Hot Springs road. Watch for traffic. The trail runs parallel to the road past the store and turns left to run down Pleasant Valley road. This is a subdivision road with occasional traffic; it is plowed and icy—tough to hook down. You will go straight off the road and then turn right on to a very well-maintained dog trail which leads 15 miles west before turning south 2 miles and dropping onto the Chena River. You are then on the river all of the way to the finish. You will cross under the Nordale Road Bridge about 5½ miles after reaching the Chena River, it's another 17 miles to downtown Fairbanks and the Banner.

Trail Notes author and two time Yukon Quest Champion John Schandelmeier drives his team along the Chena River in the 2014 Yukon Quest. [Photo by Helen Hegener/Northern Light Media]

Abandoned Klondike gold rush era buildings on Third Avenue in Dawson City.
Photo by Helen Hegener/Northern Light Media.

Chapter One ~ A Brief History of the Yukon Quest

An event like the 1,000 mile Yukon Quest generates stories and legends with almost every running, but the first race, the inaugural Yukon Quest, stands alone as the epic adventure which started it all.

On the Yukon Quest website, www.yukonquest.com, there's a somewhat abbreviated version of the history of the race, reprinted here almost in its entirety:

"In 1983, four mushers sat at a table in the Bull's Eye Saloon in Fairbanks, Alaska. The conversation turned to a discussion about a new sled dog race and "what-ifs."

• What if the race followed a historical trail?
• What if it were an international sled dog race?
• What if the race went a little longer?
• What if it even went up the Yukon River?

As early as 1976, a Fairbanks to Whitehorse sled dog race had been talked of. But it wasn't until this conversation between Roger Williams, Leroy Shank, Ron Rosser and William "Willy" Lipps that the Yukon Quest became more than an idea. The mushers named the race the "Yukon Quest" to commemorate the Yukon River, which was the historical highway of the north. The trail would trace the routes that the prospectors followed to reach the Klondike during the 1898 Gold Rush and from there to the Alaskan interior for subsequent gold rushes in the early years of the 1900s."

A somewhat longer version of the history appears in the photo-rich book by Elizabeth "Lizzie"

Martin, titled *Yukon Quest Sled Dog Race*, published in 2013 by Arcadia Publishing. In her book Elizabeth Martin recounts a little more detail about the race's colorful beginnings:

"The Yukon Quest International Sled Dog Race was born when LeRoy Shank and Roger D. Williams, along with Shank's wife, Kathleen, and some friends, got the idea for a different kind of race after running the Bull's Eye-Angel Creek 125, a 125-mile race between Bull's Eye Saloon and Angel Creek Lodge. After tossing around the idea for about three weeks, Shank decided to contact someone in Whitehorse to see if the race were possible. He called the chamber of commerce and was eventually connected with Lorrina Mitchell, who became a Yukon-based board member. She was good friends with Wendy Waters, who also joined the original Yukon board. Waters and Mitchell took care of the Whitehorse/Canada end, and a race was born."

Lorrina Mitchell had begun racing when only 16; already a veteran of sprint and mid-distance races, she signed up to run her team in the first Yukon Quest. Mary Shields was the only other woman musher in the first race. LeRoy Shank had posters made which described the rudiments and purposes of the race:

Yukon Quest Sled Dog Race
1,000 Miles Over the Gold Rush Trail
Fairbanks to Whitehorse • February 25, 1984
$15,000 in Gold - First Place
Standard long distance rules with a few notable exceptions as follows:
1. Twelve dogs starting maximum,
eight dogs starting minimum.
2. Three dogs drop limit.
3. Same sled or toboggan, start to finish.
4. Mandatory 36-hour layover at Dawson.

The purposes for which this corporation was organized are:
1. To support long distance sled dog racing and in particular to support a sled dog race of international character between Fairbanks, Alaska and Whitehorse, Yukon Territory.
2. To provide an opportunity for and encourage participation in an epic by musher and dog, without regard to the musher's sex, race, religion, national origin, background, age, vocation, or economic standing.
3. To recognize and promote the spirit that compels one to live in the Great North Land, an international spirit that knows no governmental boundaries, to bring public attention to the historic role of the Arctic Trail in the development of the North Country, and the people and animals that strove to meet its challenge.
4. To commemorate the historic dependence on man on his sled dogs for mutual survival in the Arctic Environment and to perpetuate mankind's concern for his canine companion's continued health, welfare, and development.
5. To encourage and facilitate knowledge and application of the widest variety of bush skills and practices that form the foundation of Arctic Survival.

6. To offer an experience that reflects the spirit and perseverance of the pioneers who discovered themselves in their wild search for adventure, glory, and wealth in the Frozen North.

Elizabeth Martin continued: "To get sponsors and mushers, LeRoy Shank put flyers and posters all over Fairbanks and North Pole and sent them to anyone he thought might support a Fairbanks-based long distance race, a different kind of event in which skill and know-how mattered more than money and sponsorships. It would feature the musher and the dogs on their own, with only their wits, survival skills, and gear between them and disaster, like it was 100 years ago. After a few spots on a local radio show and columns by *Fairbanks Daily News-Miner* sports writer Bob Eley, interest was sparked."

People often compare the Yukon Quest to the only other 1,000-mile sled dog race, the Iditarod. The differences between the two races were neatly summed up by Adam Killick in his book, *Racing the White Silence* (Penguin Books, 2002): "...Where the Iditarod has twenty-three checkpoints over its course, the Quest has only eight. The Quest crosses four mountain passes—all of which are steeper than the sole pass on the Iditarod—and cuts through the cold, dry heart of the Yukon and Alaska. It is run several weeks earlier than the Iditarod, beginning in early February, farther from the sun in the Earth's axial tilt. Mushers are on their own in the Quest, with the exception of one thirty-six-hour mandatory layover in Dawson City, the halfway point, where handlers can step in and provide primary care for the dogs. You are allowed only one sled: if it happens to be damaged by a rampaging moose, which happens to a musher every few years or so, it means wandering into the woods to look for replacement parts."

Mushers were advised to have a large sled, as the mandatory equipment requirements included a cold weather sleeping bag, an ax, a pair of snowshoes, a map and compass, eight booties for each dog, Yukon Quest promotional materials, and three pounds of food for each dog for every 50 miles of the race. Optional equipment included additional boots and cold weather clothing, a cookstove, dog dishes, headlamp, thermos, face mask, first aid kit, sewing kit, tent, tarp, repair kit, flashlight, batteries and more.

The morning of the first Yukon Quest, February 25, 1984, dawned clear and cold and saw twenty-six teams gathered for the inaugural start in Fairbanks. It was minus twenty degrees below zero, but the temperature was falling steadily, and by that night the teams on the trail would be facing forty below.

David "Pecos" Humphrey, from Talkeetna, was the first musher off the starting line with a dozen dogs; he was followed, in order, by Sonny Lindner with 9 dogs, Bill Cotter (10), Joe Runyan (12), Jeff King (11), Bruce Johnson (11), Nick Ericson (10), Mary Shields (10), Bob English (9), Gerald Riley (12), Jack G. Stevens (12), Harry Sutherland (10), Jack Hayden (10), Frank Turner (10), Dan Glassburn (11), David Klumb (10), Lorrina Mitchell (8), Chris Whaley (12), Ron Aldrich (12), John Two Rivers (12), Shirley Liss (8), Darryle Adkins (10), Murray Clayton (11), Wilson Sam (12), Senley Yuill (10), and Kevin Turnbough (11). Only six would scratch before Whitehorse.

In *Yukon Quest Sled Dog Race*, Elizabeth Martin described the first crossing of Eagle Summit, a name which still elicits a pause for most mushers facing the trail: "Eagle Summit.... is a 3,952-foot gap

through the White Mountains of Central Alaska. An early explorer, Hudson Stuck, wrote in 1916: 'The Eagle Summit is one of the most difficult summits in Alaska. The wind blows so fiercely that sometimes for days together its passage is almost impossible.'

"In 1984, Mother Nature threw a howling blizzard out just to shake things up. Ice formed around the dogs' and mushers' faces, so they could not see. The wind keened, piercing even the warmest furs and parkas, and got into their heads like a banshee on the prowl. Several mushers were no match for the wind, which was strong enough to knock down even the biggest mushers and their 300-pound sleds. Most mushers struggled through, but a few turned back to camp at the base in order to wait for better conditions. Both sleds and dogs took a beating, but no major injuries occurred. 'I was scared,' Bob English admitted. 'The dogs were scared.'"

The teams descended Eagle Summit into Circle Hot Springs, where the temperature dropped to minus fifty degrees and icy coats formed on the dogs and mushers alike as the humid warm air met the frigid cold. The teams raced on, across wide Medicine Lake and along the twisting Birch Creek and down onto the wide Yukon River at Circle City, then upriver 49 miles to Eagle, and another 95 miles through the jumble ice, around dangerous open leads of water, across the Canadian border and finally into historic Dawson City for a well-earned rest.

Leaving Dawson City after a 36-hour layover, the teams climbed over 4,049' King Solomon's Dome, the weathered peak that some locals still believe conceals the legendary mother lode of the 1898 Klondike gold rush. Down through the Black Hills to the Pelly River and then across a big broad country to meet the Yukon River again near the Carmacks checkpoint, 170-some miles from Whitehorse. The *Whitehorse Daily Star* would later say of the first race, "From the time the Quest started in late February to its finish in March, dog mushers battled blizzards, tough terrain, cold and warm temperatures. Many of them found the first Quest a quest to survive."

1984 Yukon Quest Results
The First Race • Inaugural Running

1. Sonny Lindner, Delta Junction
2. Harry Sutherland, Delta Junction
3. Bill Cotter, Nenana
4. Joe Runyan, Tanana
5. Jeff King, Denali Park
6. Bruce Johnson, Atlin, B.C.
7. Gerald Riley, Nenana
8. Jack Hayden, Lake Minchumina
9. Kevin Turnbough, Grand Marais, MN
10. Pecos Humphrey, Talkeetna
11. Lorrina Mitchell, Whitehorse
12. Senley Yuill, Whitehorse
13. Ron Aldrich, Willow
14. Frank Turner, Whitehorse
15. Sam Wilson, Huslia
16. Mary Shields, Schimmelpfinig Creek
17. Murray Clayton, Haines
18. Don Glassburn, Central
19. Nick Ericson, Fairbanks
20. Shirley Liss, Fairbanks
21. Daryle Adkins, Trapper Creek (scratched)
22. Bob English, Whitehorse (scratched)
23. Dave Klumb, Fairbanks (scratched)
24. Jack Stevens, Sunshine (scratched)
25. Chris Whaley, College (scratched)
26. John Two Rivers, North Pole (scratched)

Frontrunners Sonny Lindner and Joe Runyan pushed toward the Whitehorse finish line. Joe had been the first musher to leave Dawson City, but in that position he was breaking trail for all of the teams behind him, and once Sonny passed him in the Black Hills he never gave up the lead.

Trail conditions were so unseasonably warm that the trail became too soft for the teams, there was no snow in some places, and race marshal Carl Huntington and the other race officials began considering options. Elizabeth Martin titled her chapter at this point 'Hazards Mounting to the End of the Line,' and explained, "For safety reasons, officials decided to truck the teams from Carmacks to Fox Lake, bypassing about 13 miles of snowless, rocky trail and the hazardous Klondike Highway."

Hundreds of excited fans lined First Avenue in Whitehorse for the historic finish of the first Yukon Quest. Sonny Lindner's team crossed the finish line at 1:20 p.m., March 8, 1984, for an official time of twelve days and five minutes. Harry Sutherland was five hours and ten minutes behind him for second place; Bill Cotter was third, and Joe Runyan, who had led for much of the race, was fourth. Jeff King, who would later become an Iditarod legend, came in fifth.

The 1984 inaugural Yukon Quest was an unqualified success, and the race has since become a much-anticipated annual event for mushing fans the world over. It has earned the distinction of being the "Toughest Sled Dog Race in the World," and for the intrepid mushers who take on the challenge, the Yukon Quest lives up to its reputation.

"In this era of space shuttles and supersonic jets carrying people around the globe in a matter of hours, or satellite communications sending messages across continents in seconds, we tend to forget exactly how far 1,000 miles really is and what kind of an effort is required to travel it."

—John Firth, Fulda Yukon Quest (Societats-Verlag 1997)

Above: Musher Tony Angelo shakes Race Marshal Doug Grilliot's hand before departing at the 2014 start. **Right:** Cody Strathe waves on his way down the chute on Second Avenue, 2014 start. [Photos: Helen Hegener/Northern Light Media]

Chapter Two ~ Fairbanks

Golden City of the North

The Yukon Quest International Sled Dog Race begins in Fairbanks, the Golden City of the North, during even-numbered years, and travels 991 miles to Whitehorse, in the Yukon Territory. The entire downtown area bedecks itself in Yukon Quest banners, and businesses offer specials in honor of the most exciting event of winter. There are special events planned for everyone, such as the Meet the Mushers evening, a start banquet at which the mushers draw their bib numbers, and a popular pancake breakfast feed the morning of the start.

Normally the race begins on the frozen Chena River, under the Cushman Street bridge, and travels up the river through the U.S. Army's Fort Wainright and out along the Chena Hot Springs Road east of town. Occasionally, as in 2014, a few downtown streets are closed and the race begins on Second Street, dropping onto the river to continue the same route away from town.

In odd-numbered years the race ends in Fairbanks, stretching over several days as the slower, back-of-the-pack teams arrive. Whether celebrating the exciting start or the always-thrilling end of the race, Fairbanks offers a wonderful vantage point for fans of the Yukon Quest.

Above: Mushers Dave Dalton, Normand Casavant, Josh Cadzow, and Cindy Barrand at the 2010 Yukon Quest Meet the Mushers pre-race event in Fairbanks. **Below:** *A photo board of the 2010 Yukon Quest mushers.* **Right and the next two pages:** *Informal photographs of mushers at the 2010 and 2012 events. [All photos by Helen Hegener/Northern Light Media]*

Meet the Mushers

There are several popular events planned around the Fairbanks start, including a Meet the Mushers evening, a gala Start Banquet and bib drawing, and an annual Pancake Breakfast the morning of the start, all of which bring fans and mushers together for fun, friendship, and great photo opportunities.

Left to Right: Gerry Willomitzer, Terry Williams, Abbie West, Zack Steer, Brent Sass, Coleen Robertia, and Hugh Neff signing posters and pictures at the 2010 Meet the Mushers evening in Fairbanks. [Helen Hegener/Northern Light Media]

2007-2010 4X Champion Lance Mackey and 1984 Champion Sonny Lindner. [Helen Hegener/Northern Light Media]

Kristy Berington and Jake Berkowitz, 2012 Meet the Mushers. [Helen Hegener/Northern Light Media]

Left to right: Lance Mackey, Allen Moore, and Hugh Neff, 2012 Meet the Mushers. [Helen Hegener/Northern Light Media]

Jodi Bailey chats with Vern Halter at the 2012 Meet the Mushers. [Helen Hegener/Northern Light Media]

Nikolay Ettyne, Joar Leifseth Ulsom, and Jason Mackey, 2012 Meet the Mushers. [Helen Hegener/Northern Light Media]

*Above: Held in check by a snowmachine attached behind the sled, a team digs in and leaves the staging area during the 2012 Yukon Quest, in route to the start chute on the Chena River. **Left:** Below the high-rise office buildings of downtown, a team leaves the start chute, headed for Whitehorse during the 2012 race. [Both photos by Helen Hegener/Northern Light Media]*

The Start

It's a scene which has been replayed in one form or another for as long and men and dogs have traveled through this country, and you can feel the hot breath of history on the Chena River as teams start the race under some of the same buildings which mushers once passed with their sleds loaded high with freight and mail, passengers and supplies. Famous mushers have traveled these trails, men like Leonhard Seppala, Hudson Stuck, and Jujiro Wada; and more recently famous men such as Lance Mackey, Jeff King, and Martin Buser.

With a snowmachine hitched to the rear of each sled to help control the lunging huskies, and handlers with strong leads spaced at strategic points along the gangline, the excited teams advance slowly toward the start chute. The start is an emotional experience for race fans and spectators, and one can only imagine the emotions which must be coursing through each musher as he or she advances toward the moment of takeoff.

Broadcast loudly over the scene is a running commentary by the race announcer describing each team in turn as it passes under the start banner. "See those spreader bars in this musher's harness? They help distribute the weight the dogs are puling in a different way . . . ."

There's a visceral feeling to the whole event, as mushers pull their teams into the start chute to the loud cheers and best wishes of a crowd which lines both banks of the river and hangs over two large bridges, one just in front of the start chute and the other at the far end of it. Every team is sent off with loud roars of support for the grueling journey ahead.

Opposite: 2012 Champion Hugh Neff promotes literacy with his popular "Cat in the Hat" persona. *Above:* Ken Anderson poses before the 2014 start with his Quest Guest. *Left:* Normand Casavant urges the crowd to loud cheers at the 2014 start. [Helen Hegener/Northern Light Media]

Color and Spectacle Mark the Start . . .

Unlike the Iditarod 300 miles to the south, the Yukon Quest does not have a ceremonial start the day before; when the mushers and their teams leave the starting chute the clock is ticking and the race is on. That does not, however, quell the sense of ceremony and fun. Mushers and fans alike are in high spirits, and each musher has a tag sled with a rider who has won the bidding during the annual Quest Guest ride-along program, which gives fans the opportunity to ride with the musher of their choice during the first 1.5 to 2 miles of the race. The tag sleds are detached while moving, gliding to a stop as the musher continues his race.

Above: Allen Moore hugs his leaders after finishing the 2013 Yukon Quest in first place. **Right:** Moore's wife, 2000 Yukon Quest champion Aliy Zirkle, watches for the light of his headlamp. [Photos by Eric Vercammen/Northern Light Media]

Odd-Numbered Years Finish in Fairbanks

Every other year the Yukon Quest begins in Whitehorse and travels north and west to Fairbanks. The mushers say there are benefits and drawbacks to both directions, primarily based on the daunting climb and downhill slide that is Eagle Summit. Most mushers don't like seeing that formidable physical and psychological barrier near the end of their race—not that it's any easier at the beginning, but after several hundred miles the dogs and musher are both trail-weary and tired dogs are more likely to balk at the almost straight-up climb. Adam Killick described it in *Racing the White Silence*: "Eagle Summit is the Heartbreak Hill of the Yukon Quest. It's where mushers find out whether they have run the race intelligently or whether they have been running out of their league. It is a thirty-degree climb up the side of a mountain and it is reputed to be the hardest section of trail on a sled dog race anywhere."

After crossing Eagle Summit there's just one more tricky negotiation, descending Rosebud Ridge, and then the teams take a well-earned mandatory rest before traveling the floor of the Chena River Valley into Fairbanks. They're not home free though, because the valley is criss-crossed with trails and littered with distractions, and more than one musher has gotten lost in the last few miles before the finish.

It's a special kind of joy to be standing in the chute on the Chena River when a musher comes in after his thousand-mile run over the Yukon Quest trail. It's an achievement which brings a satisfied smile, and a weary but accomplished glint to a musher's eyes, knowing they've just finished the race they set out to run and have conquered the toughest trail in sled dog racing.

Left: A tired but happy Susan Rogan rests on her sled at the finish line as her partner, four-time Yukon Quest champion Hans Gatt, drives her team to their truck. She finished in 10th place in the 30th Yukon Quest, in 2013 [Helen Hegener/Northern Light Media]. *Above:* Dan Kaduce, looking weary but satisfied after finishing the 2013 Yukon Quest. *Below:* Abbie West and her leaders, finishing the 2013 race. [Both photos this page by Eric Vercammen/Northern Light Media]

The Log Cabin Yukon Quest Office

The log cabin Yukon Quest office sits downtown alongside the Chena River, right above where the race generally starts and ends on alternating years. [Photos by Eric Vercammen/Northern Light Media]

Above: National Guardsmen checkpoint volunteers watch as Iris Wood Sutton mushes her team into the Two Rivers checkpoint, at Brown Bear Campground for the 2009 race. *Right:* Mike Ellis of Team Tsuga Siberians chats with 2009 race judge Karen Ramstead of North Wapiti Kennel. [Photos by Helen Hegener/Northern Light Media]

Chapter Three ~ Two Rivers

The first checkpoint after leaving the start in Fairbanks is the Two Rivers checkpoint. When the teams are westbound from Whitehorse to Fairbanks on odd-numbered years the Two Rivers checkpoint becomes the mandatory layover point. This checkpoint has, at various times, been in several different locations around the scenic Chena River Valley, from the Brown Bear Campground to Chena Hot Springs Resort at the end of the road.

Regarding the mandatory stops, the Official Yukon Quest Race Rules for 2015 state: "In addition to Dawson City, for each team there will be a mandatory six (6) hour stop at either Braeburn or Carmacks, driver's choice. The starting time differential is added to the layover time at the chosen checkpoint. There will be a mandatory six (6) hour stop at Eagle and a mandatory six (6) hour stop at Circle, Central, or Mile 101, driver's choice. There will be a final mandatory eight (8) hour stop at Two Rivers. During each mandatory stop, every team will be evaluated by a YQI veterinarian. The driver must be present during the evaluation. Race Veterinarians will report their findings to Race Officials. Time penalties will only be served at the following designated mandatory stops: Dawson City or Two Rivers. Any time penalties assessed after Two Rivers will be added to the overall finish time."

Above: Mike Ellis's beautiful Team Tsuga Siberians, the fastest purebred Siberian husky team in the Yukon Quest and the Iditarod, race along the Chena River under the Nordale Bridge in the 2012 race. **Left:** His dogs a blur, a musher passes photographers under the Nordale bridge, 2014. [photos by Helen Hegener/Northern Light Media]

Nordale Bridge

Between Fairbanks and Two Rivers the teams pass under the bridge across the Chena River on Nordale Road. Approximately 18 miles from the Fairbanks start or finish, it's a favorite vantage point for race fans and photographers. A broad bend in the river provides a good view of the teams, and there's usually a fun sense of camaraderie amongst the fans, photographers, and handlers waiting for the teams to pass by. There is a public access boat landing on the northeast side of the bridge which provides parking, and a boat ramp which gives gradual access down to the frozen river.

Teams will be following the Yukon Quest trail markers up or down the river, depending on the direction the race is proceeding that year. On start years the teams will be closely spaced and all of them will pass this point within a few hours, but on years when the race is finishing in Fairbanks the teams will be strung out and passing under the bridge one by one or in small groups traveling together.

The area between Fairbanks and Chena Hot Springs is well-populated, and local mushers often use the same trails as the Yukon Quest mushers. This can create confusion for the mushers and their dogs, and teams sometimes lose their way, especially when traveling this section at night or after a snowfall.

Above: Brent Sass ahead of another team on Pleasant Valley Road, 2010. *Right:* Belgian Sam Deltour mushes his team up Pleasant Valley Road ahead of a car in the 2010 race. *Below:* The Pleasant Valley Store. [Helen Hegener/NLM]

Pleasant Valley Store

The Pleasant Valley Store is a well-known local landmark, race sponsor, and another favorite viewing spot for race fans and photographers. Mushers are traveling along Chena Hot Springs Road for most of the section east of the store, and west of the store the teams travel about half a mile right on Pleasant Valley Road, a local subdivision access road, providing many good opportunities for photos.

Above: Matthew Failor drives his team along Chena Hot Springs Road, 2013 Yukon Quest. [Photo by Eric Vercammen/Northern Light Media] *Left:* Hans Gatt's team swings up onto the Chena Hot Springs Road crossing in the 2010 race. *Below:* David Dalton crosses Chena Hot Springs Road in the 2010 race. [Both by Helen Hegener/Northern Light Media]

Chena Hot Springs Road

The Yukon Quest trail parallels Chena Hot Springs Road, east of Fairbanks, for several miles, offering excellent viewing opportunities for fans and photographers at the beginning of the eastbound races and the end of the race during those years when the teams are running west to Fairbanks. The race trail passes under two bridges on the frozen Chena River, at mile 24 qnd mile 28, and crosses the road itself two miles east of the Pleasant Valley Store, providing convenient vantage points appreciated by those who know where they are.

Left: Matthew Failor's dogs alert to the photographers alongside the trail ahead, 2013 race. **Above:** Dan Kaduce on the Chena River, 2013 race. **Below:** Brian Wilmshurst negotiates a turn, 2013 race. [Eric Vercammen/Northern Light Media]

Two Rivers Checkpoint

Above: For teams leaving from Fairbanks the Two Rivers checkpoint is the last stop before heading into the back country and the daunting climbs over Rosebud and Eagle Summits, but for mushers who started in Whitehorse, like Dan Kaduce in the photo above, this is where they take a mandatory eight-hour rest before the last leg to the finish line. In the photo above Dan is replacing his runner plastic. *Below:* One team resting, another getting ready to go. **Left:** The Two Rivers checkpoint cabin and a dog who has been dropped from his team. [All photos by Eric Vercammen/Northern Light Media]

All photos on these pages by Eric Vercammen/Northern Light Media

One of Dan Kaduce's Dew Claw Kennel dogs.

Raking and hauling the straw is a handler's job.

National Guard checkpoint volunteers.

Ed Hopkins getting hot water for his dogfood.

Sebastian Schnuelle writing in the media tent.

Everything is clearly marked for the trail-weary mushers.

Brian Wilmshurst gives a dog a pill.

The dropped dogs are not happy to be left behind.

Left: Mushers' drop bags contain food, clothes, batteries, gear and other items the mushers will need on the trail.
Above: The checkpoint at Mile 101. *Below:* The dogs know when to rest. [All by Eric Vercammen/Northern Light Media]

Chapter Four ~ Mile 101

At the bottom of Eagle Summit

The third checkpoint outbound from Fairbanks sits at the bottom of the climb to Eagle Summit, for many mushers the most dreaded part of the trail. In his classic 1916 book, *Ten Thousand Miles with a Dog Sled*, Hudson Stuck, Archdeacon of the Yukon and one of the first white men to navigate the summit with a dogteam, wrote, "The Eagle Summit is one of the most difficult summits in Alaska. The wind blows so fiercely that sometimes for days together its passage is almost impossible. ... The snow smothers up everything on the lee side of the hill, and the end of every storm presents a new surface and an altered route. ... there is no easier pass and no way around."

A mail team struggles over Eagle Summit in 1939. Photographer unknown.

A Perilous Part of the Mail Route

In the May 12, 2012 issue of the *Fairbanks Daily News-Miner*, David A. James reviewed a book by William S. Schneider, professor emeritus and retired curator of oral history at University of Alaska Fairbanks, titled *On Time Delivery* (2012, University of Alaska Press, Fairbanks}. Describing the historic mail routes of Interior Alaska, James wrote, "Perhaps the most perilous was the old Fairbanks-Circle Trail, which included Eagle Summit. Now part of the Yukon Quest route, this steep climb noted for extreme winds and deadly cold temperatures is considered the most treacherous part of that race. But while today's mushers traverse it once on their way to the finish line, 80 years ago mail haulers repeatedly crossed it all winter long."

Airlifted off Eagle Summit

In the early years of the race the trail ran directly on the Steese Highway across the pass, avoiding the treacherous mountain summit the trail follows today.

In a 2011 article for the *Fairbanks Daily News-Miner* titled "Eagle Summit draws criticism from some as a dangerous route for Yukon Quest mushers," writer Matias Saari described this section of the trail:

"The route from Central rises gradually and approaches Eagle Summit for about two hours. Once at the base of Eagle Summit, the actual climb involves one gradual ascent followed by a saddle and a brief drop before the crux: an exceedingly steep 'headwall' climb of at least 250 vertical feet in less than 200 yards."

Saari noted that the approach from the other direction was not very easy for the mushers to navigate either: "Eagle Summit poses the biggest challenge in the Whitehorse-to-Fairbanks direction (run in odd-numbered years), but that doesn't mean the approach from Mile 101 is easy (run in even-numbered years). The climb that way is less daunting, but then mushers are treated to what can be a harrowing ride down the headwall to begin their descent toward Central. That direction also featured a rescue of several mushers and their teams by military helicopter after they were stranded on the stormy summit in 2006."

In an article for *Mushing Magazine*, Jillian Rogers described the airlift ordeal:

"Around 5 p.m. on Sunday, February 12, fat snowflakes started to fall at the Mile 101 dog drop, signaling bad weather atop Eagle Summit. As the leaders .... departed for the Central checkpoint, rookie mushers rested their teams at the dog drop until after dark. The winds on the summit picked up to hurricane force, and, coupled with fresh snow, created a whiteout in which mushers couldn't even see the dogs in front of their sleds. [Lance] Mackey was third into Central after clearing the summit and quickly told the group of fans and media that he's never been that scared in his life. [Hans] Gatt was the first to arrive in Central.

"'Someone's going to die up there tonight,' Gatt said, much to the shock of onlookers."

By the next morning, six mushers and seven dog teams were lost in the blizzard on Eagle Summit; the seventh team belonged to a Yukon Quest 300 musher who lost control of his dog team and caught a ride with another musher. Volunteers on snowmachines left from Central in an attempt to locate the lost mushers, but the weather forced the rescuers back to the checkpoint. By early afternoon, planes and helicopters owned by the US military and state troopers were called in to pluck the terrified group off the mountain. After a search that included a Blackhawk helicopter and infrared technology, all the racers and their dogs were rescued and back at the Mile 101 dog drop. Race marshal Mike McCowan commented, "A lot of people risked their lives today."

Wild RIde Down Eagle Summit

Veteran Yukon Quest musher Michelle Phillips shared her own story about Eagle Summit - that same year - in her 2012 book, *1,000 Mile Sled Dog Journal – My Yukon Quest Story*:

"We flew down this hill and then the trail went over to the left, but my team decided to travel straight down the mountain! I couldn't stop them and a lot of the markers had been run over so I wasn't really sure where to go. We flew over ice and rocks. At one point I had two snow hooks and one bounced off my sled and jammed into the ground. I was traveling so fast my sled kept going and the line from the snow hook snapped my brush bow. I had to cut the line to my snow hook and give it up to the mountain...."

Michelle eventually made it down safely, and hugged each of her dogs to celebrate, although she admitted "They all looked totally freaked out and I couldn't blame them!"

A 2014 Yukon Quest 300 musher a mile or so before the Mile 101 checkpoint. [Helen Hegener/Northern Light Media]

A 2014 Yukon Quest 300 musher along the trail to the Mile 101 checkpoint. [Helen Hegener/Northern Light Media]

The Mile 101 checkpoint is a busy place when mushers arrive. [Helen Hegener/Northern Light Media]

Peter Kamper has been a volunteer at the Mile 101 checkpoint for many years. [Helen Hegener/Northern Light Media]

The mushers find good food and a warm place to sleep here. [Eric Vercammen/Northern Light Media]

There are sleeping bunks and plenty of food at Mile 101. [Helen Hegener/Northern Light Media]

The dogs welcome the chance to get some sleep. [Eric Vercammen/Northern Light Media]

Straw spread over the snow gives the dogs a warm, comfortable bed [Eric Vercammen/Northern Light Media]

Above: Kristy Berington crosses Eagle Summit, 2012 race. *Below and Right*: Mushers and their teams appear small against the seemingly limitless Eagle Summit landscapes. [All photos these pages by Scott Chesney/Talespin Media]

Above and below: *The road over Eagle Summit crosses a 3,652-foot gap in the White Mountains; the dog teams cross over a nearby ridge. The road can be daunting when ice fog closes in, as in the photo on the right. When conditions warrant it the Highway Department closes the road for indefinite periods of time. [All photos: Helen Hegener/Northern Light Media]*

Left: *Mike Ellis drives his Team Tsuga Siberians down the Steese Highway and into Central.* **Above:** *Central Corner is the checkpoint. The orange, silver, and black stakes are the Yukon Quest trail markers. [Helen Hegener/Northern Light Media]*

Chapter Five ~ Central

Mushing Down Main Street

After traveling down the steep slopes from Eagle Summit and across the foothills of the White Mountains, the teams come out of the woods and onto the Steese Highway just before it reaches the small community of Central. At this point the Yukon Quest trail stakes run right down the highway for about a mile and into the checkpoint at Central Corner, a local gas-cafe-motel-grocery store which sits near where the original Central House was built more than one hundred and twenty years ago.

That first roadhouse, which was built around 1894, was named Central House because it was centrally located where the primitive pack trail from Circle, on the Yukon River, crossed Crooked Creek on its way to the Circle Mining District operations at Birch, Mammoth, Mastodon, and Preacher Creeks, gold-bearing streams which tumbled out of the foothills of the White Mountains. The roadhouse became the center of a small community of people who settled there and provided food and shelter to travelers and support services to nearby miners. In 1906, the Alaska Road Commission began construction of a wagon road to replace the primitive pack trail from Circle to the Birch Creek mining operations, and by 1908 that road construction reached Central.

Above: As another musher's team rests in the foreground, Mike Ellis parks his frost-covered team with help from a handler.
Right: A race judge stands on the brake while a musher shows his required race gear. [Helen Hegener/Northern Light Media]

The original roadhouse burned to the ground and was rebuilt in the mid-1920s. A post office was established in 1925, and in 1927, the road link to Fairbanks was completed. The road was named the Steese Highway in honor of General James Steese, a former president of the Alaska Road Commission. Mining continued until the beginning of World War II, when most young men joined the military and left Alaska to fight on foreign shores.

After the war, a few miners returned to Central, but mining declined through the 1950s and 60s. Activity increased again in the mid-1970s with the rise in gold prices. In 1978, the Circle Mining District was the most active in Alaska, with 65 gold mining operations employing over 200 people. The 2000 census listed 134 people living in Central, but by 2010 that number had dropped to 96.

Today Central is known for gold mining and the Yukon Quest, and for the historic Arctic Circle Hot Springs Resort, eight miles south of the community. The Yukon Quest mushers leave Central on the Circle Hot Springs Road, and pass by the resort just before starting the downhill run to Medicine Lake. After crossing the lake the teams will head out into the broad hilly country between Central and Circle City, following the curlicued Birch Creek north to the village of Circle, where the eastbound teams will meet the Yukon River.

Central Corner, Yukon Quest checkpoint. [Eric Vercammen/Northern Light Media]

A friendly crowd of mushers, handlers, race officials, vets, media and fans. [Helen Hegener/Northern Light Media]

Emily Schwing interviews Ken Anderson for KUAC. [Helen Hegener/Northern Light Media]

While waiting for his dinner, Mike Ellis chats with the media. [Helen Hegener/Northern Light Media]

A musher signs in at the Central checkpoint. [Helen Hegener/Northern Light Media]

Updating the leader board at Central Corner. [Helen Hegener/Northern Light Media]

Misha Petersen leaving the Central checkpoint, 2012 Yukon Quest. [Helen Hegener/Northern Light Media]

Trail sweeps at Central Corner, 2013 Yukon Quest. [Eric Vercammen/Northern Light Media]

Arctic Circle Hot Springs [photos by Helen Hegener/Northern Light Media

Arctic Circle Hot Springs

The Arctic Circle Hot Springs Resort was the second checkpoint in the first running of the Yukon Quest in 1984. The hot springs, known to the local Athabascan Indians long before the gold rush, were 'discovered' in 1893 by prospector William Great, reportedly hunting moose. They were homesteaded in 1907 and developed into a resort by Franklin and Emma Leach, who grew acres of vegetables.

The Leaches built the classic bay-windowed 22-room hotel in the 1930s, as explained by Ray Bonnell in a 2013 article for the *Fairbanks Daily News-Miner*: "They hired local sourdough Billy Bowers to oversee construction, and work on the hotel began in March 1930. Some accounts say most construction materials came by river to Circle and then by wagon to the springs. However, in a 1970's taped interview, Emma Leach said the logs used for lumber were felled at Medicine Lake several miles northeast of the springs, and that additional lumber was trucked from Fairbanks. The hotel was completed by that fall."

Sign on the road to Circle. [Helen Hegener/NLM]

At Birch Hill on the Steese Highway. [Helen Hegener/NLM]

A few miles from Central a musher takes his team off the road as a car approaches. [Helen Hegener/Northern Light Media]

In 2012 Misha Pedersen, a musher from Prague in the Czech Republic, took Jim and Bonnie Foster's team of Moon Run Kennel retired sled dogs from Fairbanks to Whitehorse. On Yukon Quest website, Misha answered the question, "What do you love most about running sled dogs?" with the reply, "They are like three musketeers, one for all and all for one." Crossing Eagle Summit, a dog named Riot broke loose and disappeared, jeopardizing Misha's chances of finishing the race, but she was caught by a Yukon Quest 300 musher, Ed Abrahamson, who came into the Central checkpoint with Riot in his team. As this constituted no outside-the-race interference, Misha was able to put Riot back into her team and continue the race. Misha and the Moon Run dogs finished in 17th place, and Bonnie Foster, who, along with her son Randy, was handling for Misha during the race, wrote in her journal: "For sure, it has been a hell of a journey with highs and lows and sometimes just pure desperation and some darn good luck." [Helen Hegener/Northern Light Media]

*Above: The fire hall serves as the Circle City checkpoint. **Right:** Beyond a door decorated with local schoolkids' artwork, Sebastian Schnuelle gets in some computer time at the fire hall, 2014 race. [Helen Hegener/Northern Light Media]*

Chapter Six ~ Circle City

The Checkpoint at the End of the Road

The Circle checkpoint is at the end of the Steese Highway, where the frozen Yukon River becomes the trail on and off again for the rest of the race. The checkpoint is housed in the local fire hall, where picnic tables for feeding the mushers and officials are set up alongside the town's single firetruck. Over the course of the race the mushers drape coats, hats, mittens and more on the firetruck's mirrors and ladder, and they often sleep atop, under, and all around the firetruck, even though there is a quiet room set aside for them.

Two blocks away, the modern, modular Circle school offers sleeping space for handlers, the media, and others in the school gymnasium, and the enterprising schoolkids sell delicious hot breakfasts, lunches, and dinners to raise funds for their annual school field trips. There is a well-used laundromat with hot showers, and one general store which doubles as a miniature museum, with gold rush relics, antiques from a bygone era, and a collection of interesting miscellany which attracts almost as many fascinated browsers as bona fide shoppers.

***Left:** The Rasmussen House, a unique two-story log cabin, was built in 1909 by freighter Nels Rasmussen. **Above:** At night you can see the mushers' headlamps coming from five miles up the Yukon River. [Helen Hegener/Northern Light Media]*

On the Banks of the Yukon River

Circle (also known as Circle City) was established in 1894 when gold was discovered on Birch Creek, in the nearby White Mountains. Before the 1897 Klondike Gold Rush, Circle was the largest mining town on the Yukon River, with a population of over 700 people, and it was a regular stop for steamboats plying the river. Often referred to as the "Paris of the North," Circle City's log cabins reportedly stretched for a mile and a half along the riverfront.

The town served as an unloading point for supplies shipped up the Yukon River from the Bering Sea and then freighted overland to the gold mining camps around interior Alaska. The town boasted an Alaska Commercial Company store, a library, a school, a hospital, a newspaper, a mill, and more. Several federal officials were based there, including a United States commissioner, a town marshal, a customs inspector, a tax collector and a postmaster. There was reportedly even an opera house for more genteel entertainment than the several often raucous dance halls in town.

After the gold discoveries in the Klondike in 1897 and Nome in 1899, Circle lost much of its population. A few miners stayed in the area, but the town never reached its pre-Klondike heyday numbers again. Mining in the area has continued into the 21st century, but much of that activity is based closer to Central, and today most of the residents of Circle are Athabascan.

Teams in the dog lot at the Circle City checkpoint. [Helen Hegener/Northern Light Media]

Colleen Robertia arrives in Circle City, 2009 race. [Helen Hegener/Northern Light Media]

Dogs lean into their harnesses to go to the Circle City dog lot. [Helen Hegener/Northern Light Media]

Yukon Quest 300 musher Heidi Sutter dishes food for her dogs. [Helen Hegener/Northern Light Media]

Inside the fire hall checkpoint at Circle City. [Helen Hegener/Northern Light Media]

Trailbreaker John Schandelmeier chats with KUAC reporter Emily Schwing, 2011. [Helen Hegener/Northern Light Media]

Race officials check weather, standings, and trail reports via the Internet. [Helen Hegener/Northern Light Media]

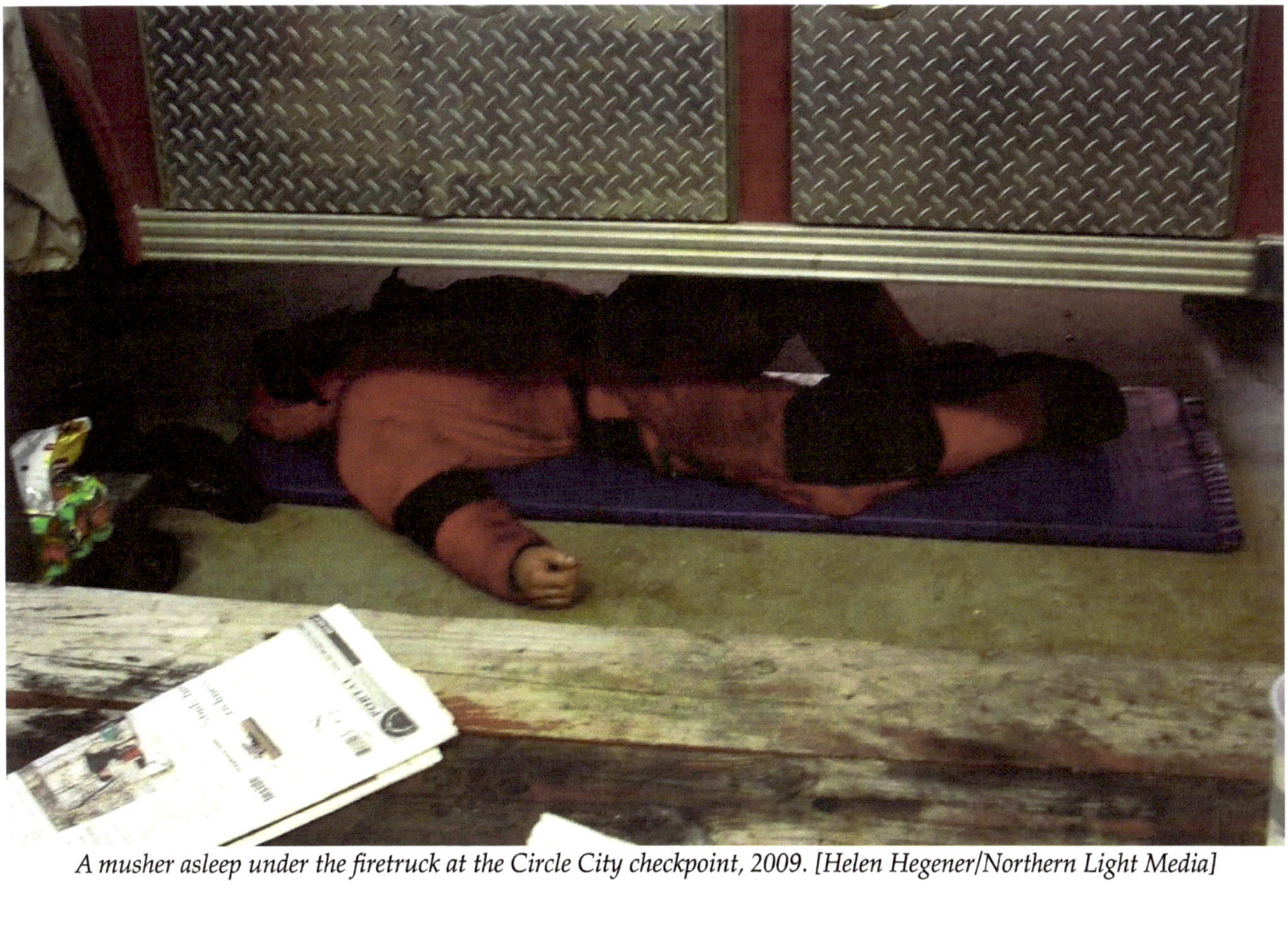

A musher asleep under the firetruck at the Circle City checkpoint, 2009. [Helen Hegener/Northern Light Media]

Drop bags at the Circle City checkpoint, 2009 race. [Helen Hegener/Northern Light Media]

Brent Sass leaves the Circle City checkpoint, 2009 race. [Helen Hegener/Northern Light Media]

Changing sled runner plastic. [Helen Hegener/Northern Light Media]

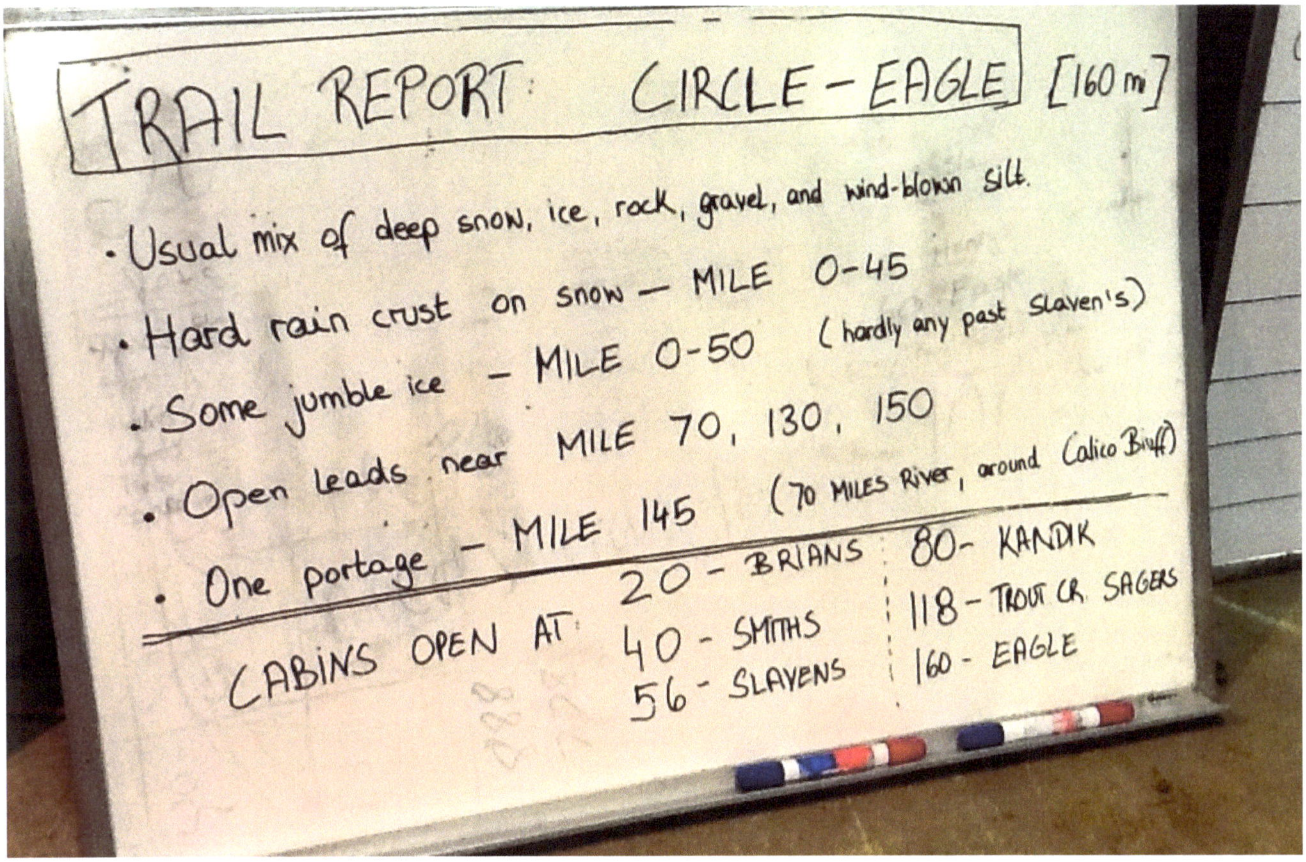

Reports on the trail ahead at the Circle City checkpoint, 2014 race. [Helen Hegener/Northern Light Media]

Above: Ben Downing's Mail Teams in front of post office at Eagle, Alaska, circa 1900. [Photo by C.L. Andrews, from Alaska State Library, ASL-P45-1031] *Left:* Ed Hopkins' Yukon Quest dogs, 2013 race. [Eric Vercammen/Northern Light Media]

Chapter Seven ~ Eagle

The Remotest Checkpoint

Eagle, another gold rush era town, is the only Yukon Quest checkpoint which cannot be reached by road in the winter. Situated approximately 160 miles north of Circle via the Yukon River, and around 150 miles from the next checkpoint at Dawson City, also via the Yukon River, Eagle is at the end of the Taylor Highway, a seasonal road which is usually covered in snow from late fall to early spring.

There's a colorful description of Eagle in Adam Killick's classic 2002 book about the Yukon Quest, *Racing the White Silence*: "Eagle, which sits on a sandy deposit at a windy, sweeping bend in the Yukon River, is home to some fishermen, a tourist paddlewheel replica called the *Yukon Queen*, a motel, a bed-and-breakfast, and not much else."

After describing the town's namesake, a basalt cliff known as Eagle Bluff, as "one of the most recognizable landmarks on the Yukon Quest trail," Killick admitted there was a bit more to the town, which "boasts a pool hall, two landing strips, a laundromat…" and two schools, including an old one-room school which serves as the Yukon Quest checkpoint each year. Many of the buildings from the Gold Rush years are preserved as part of the Eagle Historic District, a National Historic Landmark.

Above: Historic Biederman Camp on the banks of the Yukon River, circa 1930s. [UAF Archives, George Beck Collection]
Right: A musher and his team departing Frank Slaven's Roadhouse in the Yukon-Charley Rivers National Preserve during the 2005 Yukon Quest sled dog race. [National Park Service [Public domain], via Wikimedia Commons]

Slaven's, Biederman's, and Trout Creek

There are several cabins which serve as hospitality stops and one which is an official dog drop between Circle City and Eagle.

Slaven's Cabin, also called Slaven's Roadhouse, is a public-use facility in the Yukon-Charley Rivers National Preserve, located on the Yukon River, 60 miles upriver from Circle. Miner Frank Slaven, who arrived in the area in 1905, enlisted friends to help him build the roadhouse in 1932. It is listed on the National Register of Historic Places and serves as an official dog drop for the Yukon Quest.

Eighteen miles farther is Biederman's Cabin, the former home of Charlie Biederman, who was one of the last surviving dogsled mail carriers in the United States. His father, Ed Biederman, also delivered the mail via dog team between Eagle and Circle. The 160-mile route took six days one way and, after a rest day, six days back. Biederman did this thirteen times each winter, covering 4000 miles of rough trail. In 1937 the *Washington Daily News* correspondent Ernie Pyle wrote of Ed Biederman, "The things Biederman has been through would fill a book. I suppose no man knows more about sled dogs, or winter weather, or making his way alone in wild country."

Another cabin is Trout Creek, at the mouth of the Yukon River tributary of that name, 28 miles from the Eagle checkpoint. More cabins are listed in John Schandelmeier's *Trail Notes for Mushers*.

Above: A load of mail at Eagle. [Date, photographer unknown] Right: Ice fog enshrouds everything, making travel dangerous on the river, where there can be leads of open water. [Helen Hegener/Northern Light Media]

80 Sled Dogs and A Legendary Mail Carrier

Sled dog teams played a huge role in the history of Eagle, as mail, freight, passengers and other loads passed through the town on a regular basis for many years. The town was formally organized by miners in 1897, and by the following year the population had soared to 1,700. The new town boasted four major trading companies, a post office, a newspaper, and a federal court presided over by Judge James Wickersham. An Army post, Fort Egbert, was built nearby in 1901, and it included 19 kennels housing 80 sled dogs which helped survey and construct the Signal Corps' Washington-Alaska Military Cable and Telegraph System (WAMCATS) across Alaska from 1900 through 1904, linking the Army's far-flung posts with each other and with the contiguous United States.

It was the mail carriers whose exploits would become the stuff of legends, as men like Percy DeWolfe, Ben Downing, and Adolph 'Ed' Biederman risked their lives to carry the U.S. Mail along the Yukon River. Arriving in the Yukon Territory during the gold rush of 1898, the intrepid Percy DeWolfe won the contract to carry the mail from Dawson City to Eagle in 1910. He carried the mail for almost forty years with a boat and a team of horses in the summer, and by dogteam in the winter, following a string of roadhouses located at intervals along the route, regardless of the sometimes treacherous weather conditions. Today the Percy DeWolfe Memorial Mail Race, begun in 1977 and running from Dawson City to Eagle, honors this legendary musher and mail carrier.

The Handlers' Trail: A Long Drive

While the mushers are making their way along the Yukon River to Dawson City, the handlers, media, and many others are making their own trek by road. As team after team headed out onto the frozen Yukon River from Circle City, the handlers driving the big dog trucks set off in the opposite direction for a 1,000-mile drive to Dawson City, because the mushers were now in territory only accessible by air, snowmachine, or, of course, dogsled.

The support teams tackle a long two-day drive, over icy mountains, through blowing snow and howling winds, but also through some of the most spectacular scenery to be found anywhere. From Circle City they'll backtrack along the Steese Highway to Fairbanks, re-crossing Eagle Summit and Rosebud Summit, to Fairbanks, where they'll turn south and east onto the Alaska Highway.

The road passes through many small communities between Fairbanks and the Canadian border: North Pole, Salcha, Delta Junction, Dot Lake, Tok -- a major junction where the Glenn Highway heads south to Anchorage -- and then only the occasional lodge, most closed for the winter, until they reach the small border community of Beaver Creek, Yukon Territory. There's not much there... the Canadian customs office, a couple of lodges with gas pumps out front; the town's population is only 120 or so.

Leaving Beaver Creek, the Alaska Highway heads into the remote territory north of the Wrangell, Kluane, and Nutzotin mountain ranges, an area long notorious for some of the coldest winter temperatures on record. It's beautiful country, crossing the glacial White and Donjek Rivers, and offering spectacular views to the south of the Icefield Ranges of the St. Elias Mountains, the highest in Canada, with seven peaks over 16,000 feet, including Canada's highest mountain, Mount Logan, at 19,545 feet.

The highway winds around the edge of the mostly frozen Kluane Lake, the largest in the Yukon Territory at over 150 square miles. The falling-in log cabins of Silver City, a 1904 trading post, roadhouse, and North West Mounted Police barracks, sits on the eastern shore of the lake. The highway crosses 3,293-foot Boutiller Summit and drops into Haines Junction under a panoramic view of the skyscraping Auriol Range, then finally turns north toward Whitehorse, 100 miles away.

Just before reaching Whitehorse, actually skirting the edge of the city limits, Yukon Highway 2, also known as the North Klondike Highway or the Klondike Loop, heads off to the left and soon crosses the Takhini River bridge, a favorite viewing spot when the teams cross under it in a week or so. This is where the drivers once again meet the Yukon River -- it's off to the right -- and they'll more or less follow it all the way to Dawson City, 323 miles away. The highway runs alongside the 40-mile-long Lake Laberge, which Robert Service made famous in his epic poem, "The Cremation of Sam McGee":"The Northern Lights have seen queer sights, but the queerest they ever did see, was that night on the marge of Lake Laberge I cremated Sam McGee."

Lake Laberge is actually just a widening of the Yukon River, but farther along the road passes Fox Lake, Little Fox Lake, and Braeburn Lake -- and then the last official checkpoint before the finish of the Yukon Quest, Braeburn Lodge. The dogtrucks roll on by for now, and pass checkpoints and dog drops along the way... Carmacks, McCabe Creek, Pelly Crossing, Stepping Stone, Scroggie Creek... and finally, the historic Klondike gold rush town of Dawson City, where they'll set up camps for their teams.

The trail-weary mushers will undoubtedly be happy to see them.

The Alaska Highway crosses Christmas Creek, east of Kluane Lake. [Helen Hegener/Northern Light Media]

Left: *Lance Mackey drives his team up the Yukon River, 2008 Yukon Quest. [Helen Hegener/Northern Light Media]*
Above: *Abbie West and her team arrive in Dawson City, 2012 race. [Scott Chesney/Talespin Media]*

Chapter Eight ~ Dawson City

A Mandatory Layover

At the height of the Klondike Gold Rush, which started in 1896, Dawson was a thriving city of 40,000, the largest city north of San Francisco and west of Winnipeg, and those glamorous Gold Rush roots of this frontier town are still clearly visible. The building facades, fancy dormers and gingerbread details have not been added on for the sake of increasing tourist appeal; those are for the most part the real deal, dating from before the turn of the century.

Prior to the 2015 race mushers would take a mandatory 36-hour layover here, but new rules dropped that to a 24-hour mandatory layover. Dawson City is the only checkpoint where mushers may receive outside help with their teams. The campground across the Yukon River becomes the staging area for the race, with each team assigned a campsite. The handlers, most of whom drove nearly 1,500 miles to arrive ahead of their musher, will have set up the camp and dog shelter before his arrival.

Rest, thorough vet checks, time differential adjustments, sled repairs, and rejuvenation for both mushers and their dogs are the goals, and after their layover each musher drives his or her team back onto the ice of the Yukon River and continues the journey to either Whitehorse or Fairbanks.

While the race judges, veterinarians, media personnel, and handlers driving the big dogtrucks arrive in Dawson City via the Klondike Highway from Whitehorse and beyond, the mushers come into town on the frozen Yukon River, often exhausted from having fought for trail through treacherously jumbled slabs of river ice. [Helen Hegener/Northern Light Media]

The mushers camp is at the territorial campground across the Yukon River. [Helen Hegener/Northern Light Media]

During the 2008 race this 10' tall ice inuksuk welcomed mushers to Dawson City. There was a second inuksuk about half a mile upriver, providing a visual reference point for the trail. Usually a stone landmark used by peoples of the Arctic region, an area with few natural landmarks, the inuksuit have ancient roots in Inuit culture. [Helen Hegener/Northern Light Media]

Dog trucks crossing the frozen Yukon River to the campground, 2008. [Helen Hegener/Northern Light Media]

A musher's camp at the territorial campground. [Helen Hegener/Northern Light Media]

A musher's sled. [Helen Hegener/Northern Light Media]

Hard-working dogs enjoy a well-deserved rest at Dawson City. [Helen Hegener/Northern Light Media]

A pile of worn dog booties. [Helen Hegener/Northern Light Media]

Mushers listen to reports on the trail ahead, 2008 race. [Helen Hegener/Northern Light Media]

Paige Drobney arrives in Dawson City, 2012 race. [Scott Chesney/Talespin Media]

An empty gangline leads to a sled at rest in the campground. [Helen Hegener/Northern Light Media]

At the Dawson City mushers' campground. [Scott Chesney/Talespin Media]

Left and above: Yukon Quest veterinarians examine and assess each dog thoroughly at the Dawson City checkpoint, making sure they are fit and ready to travel the remaining miles of the race. [Helen Hegener/Northern Light Media]

Veterinary Care

The Yukon Quest veterinary team is responsible for the most important part of the race, the health of the hundreds of dogs who will run the nearly one-thousand-mile trail. The team of veterinarians assembled by the Yukon Quest International Sled Dog Race each winter hails from many parts of the world, and each team member brings many years of experience with sled dogs to the race.

While veterinarians are available at every checkpoint and dog drop on the trail, Dawson City, the halfway point in this epic journey, is one of three mandatory vet checks during the race, and consists of a veterinary assessment of each dog's circulatory system, including heart rates and sounds; hydration status and body weight; respiratory sounds; gastrointestinal tract; attitude and appetite; and last but not least, a thorough orthopedic exam. Each musher is required to carry their team veterinary records at all times, and loss of these records will incur a stiff penalty.

The Yukon Quest is renowned as a race where dog care is of primary importance, and the teamwork between mushers and veterinarians assures the well-being of the canine athletes.

A National Historic Site, the Keno is one of only three Yukon sternwheelers that survive in good condition, from a fleet that numbered at least 250 in total during the century between 1855 and 1955. [Scott Chesney/Talespin Media]

Gold Rush City

The Klondike Gold Rush brought an estimated 50,000 prospectors to northwestern Canada between 1896 and 1899, when the discovery of gold on the beaches of Nome prompted an abrupt exodus down the Yukon River. But during its heyday the Gold Rush city gained a reputation which still resonates.

Founded at the confluence of the Klondike and Yukon Rivers, the town was named for the noted Canadian geologist George M. Dawson, who explored and mapped the area in 1897. The town grew from a population of 500 in 1896 to around 40,000 people by the summer of 1898. Town characters loomed larger than life, and stories of the "Paris of the North," the biggest city west of Winnipeg and north of San Francisco, would fill entire books.

John Balzar wrote about Dawson City in *Yukon Alone*: "…The capital of the Klondike, with its Wild West facades and stovepipe chimneys, is recognizable from the black-and-white photographs of the Gold Rush. Saloon doors still swing until late and hairy men stagger forth bleary-eyed and broke. Music wafts down the frozen streets. Some old clapboard buildings have been slapped with fresh paint while others, bare wood, sag into the permafrost. Dog teams still ride into down on dreary winter days and stop on Front Street, and you have to wait until the hoarfrost melts from the newcomer's face to see if it's someone you know. Merchants are proud to post signs saying that they accept payment in gold dust. Indeed, gold still rules in these hills–the tailings of the old claims are being turned over and worked for the third time. Fewer nuggets are found, but there's plenty of powder gold…"

Gold Rush-era buildings on Third Street, Dawson City. [Helen Hegener/Northern Light Media]

The Canadian Bank of Commerce, where Bard of the Yukon Robert Service worked in 1908. He lived in a log cabin while writing classics such as 'The Spell of the Yukon' and 'The Cremation of Sam McGee.' [Helen Hegener/Northern Light Media]

Left: A campfire brings people together for warmth and camaraderie on the trail. [Scott Chesney/Talespin Media]
Above: A brightly burning fire warms the waiting handlers, volunteers, and others. [Helen Hegener/Northern Light Media]

Mushers

"I wander across the ice bridge over the Yukon to the west side of the river. Here, in a thicket of oversize spruce, campfires crackle. Mushers and dog handlers have retreated from the raucous town to the woods, where they feel at home.

"The murmur of conversation in inconsequential, and timeless. The weather, the standings, the trail behind, the trail ahead, old stories from other trails, how the dogs are eating, how they are shitting. Men and women laugh, and pause in long silences as people do around campfires, poking sticks into the flames and watching the coals melt into the snow. They brag about their good dogs, and bitch because they don't have enough of them. Hardly anybody, apparently, has leaders worth a damn, though I wonder how any team has made it this far if that's so.

"I look at the faces. Tough. Reddened even in firelight. Their hands are scabbed and chapped. Lips are cracked. Their insulated trail overalls are smeared with dog food; their white rubber bunny boots have grown gray and scuffed, and the laces dangle loosely. For camp chores, these dog people wear fleece work gloves that are filthy, stiff, and scorched. Even with many hours of Dawson City rest, their eyes are red and puffy. Altogether content, I'd say."

John Balzar, in *Yukon Alone*

The Klondike River just south of Dawson City. [Helen Hegener/Northern Light Media]

Tintina ('Chief') Trench, an important geologic landmark in the Yukon Territory. [Helen Hegener/Northern Light Media]

The Stewart River bridge at Stewart Crossing. [Helen Hegener/Northern Light Media]

The bridge over the Pelly River at the Pelly Crossing checkpoint. [Helen Hegener/Northern Light Media]

Left: The St. James log church, built of locally grown trees, completed in 1964. *Above:* The community center served as the 2008 checkpoint. *Below:* David Bennett, the Pelly Crossing checkpoint manager. [Helen Hegener/Northern Light Media]

Chapter Nine ~ Pelly Crossing

Home of the Selkirk First Nation

The Pelly Crossing checkpoint, located where the Klondike Highway crosses the Pelly River, has always been notable for the warm hospitality provided by the residents of this Selkirk First Nations community. Established as a ferry crossing and highway construction camp in 1950, when the Klondike Highway was built between Whitehorse and Dawson City, the community provides a welcome stop for mushers after a long and arduous journey from Dawson City.

Flowing from an unnamed glacier in the Mackenzie Mountains and named for a governor of the Hudson's Bay Company, the Pelly River is one of two major headwaters of the Yukon River (the other is the Stewart River). The river was named by Robert Campbell in honor of Sir John Henry Pelly, governor of the Hudson's Bay Company. The restored Hudson's Bay Company trading post of Fort Selkirk is at the confluence of the Pelly and Yukon Rivers.

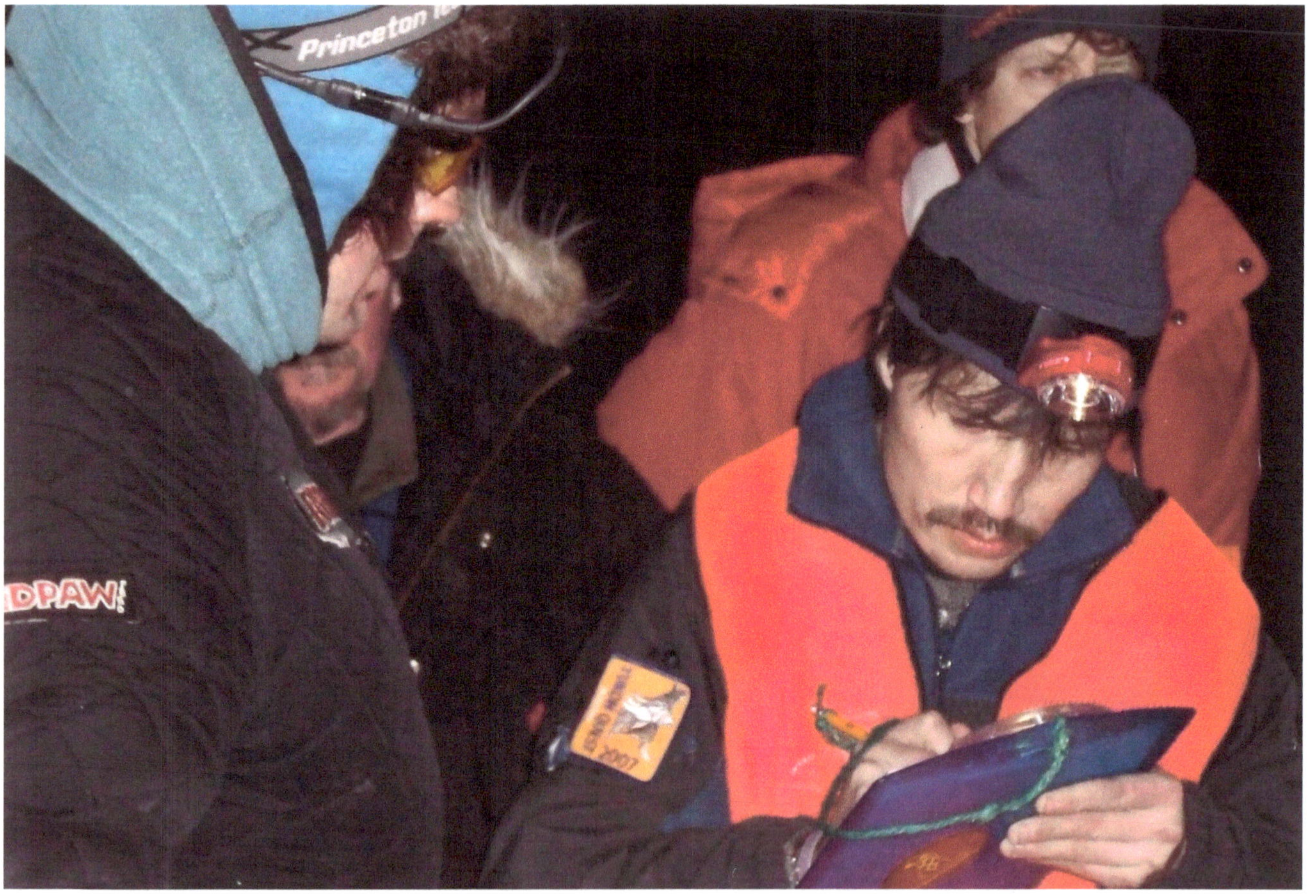

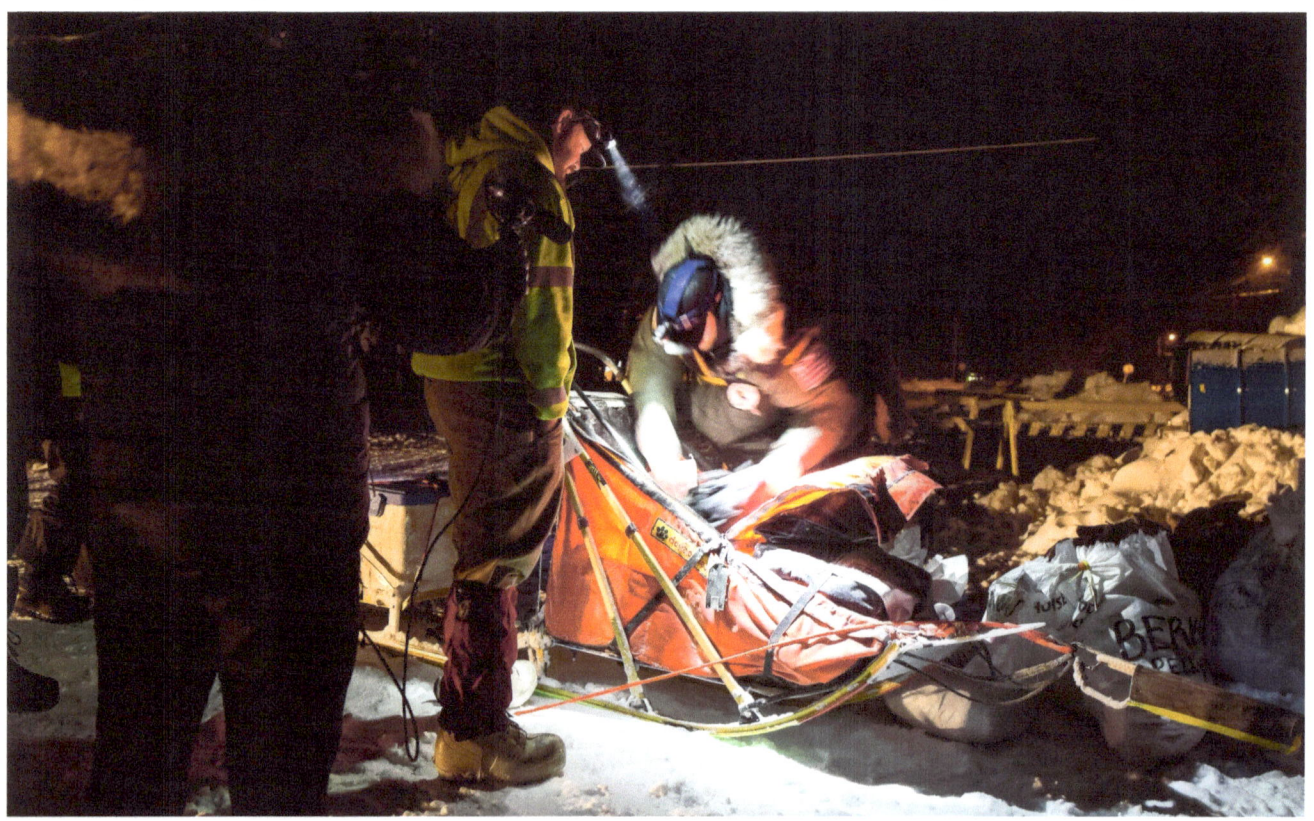

Checkpoint manager David Bennett checks in Ken Anderson, 2008 race. [Helen Hegener/Northern Light Media]

Jake Berkowitz tends to his team at the Pelly Crossing checkpoint, 2013 race. [Scott Chesney/Talespin Media]

Lance Mackey empties his drop bag, 2008 race. [Helen Hegener/Northern Light Media]

A vet checks over the dogs at Pelly Crossing, 2013 race. [Scott Chesney/Talespin Media]

Above: The Carmacks community recreation center serves as the Carmacks checkpoint. *Below:* "Mushers sleeping - Quiet Please" on a door at the community center. [Helen Hegener/Northern Light Media] *Right:* Hugh Neff's team drops over the steep bank and onto the broad Yukon River at Carmacks during the 2013 race. [Scott Chesney/Talespin Media]

Chapter Ten ~ Carmacks

Named for George Washington Carmack

Carmacks, a village at the confluence of the Nordenskiold and Yukon rivers, is home to the Little Salmon/Carmacks First Nation, a Northern Tutchone-speaking people. The area around Carmacks, including the rich Nordenskiold River, was a favored fishing and trading spot with trails fanning out in all directions.

The settlement was named for George Washington Carmack, who built a trading post and traded with the local people before discovering coal nearby and opening a coal mine in the south bank of the Yukon River in 1893. Three years later Carmack, along with Skookum Jim and Tagish Charlie, discovered gold near Dawson City, starting the Klondike Gold Rush.

The Yukon Quest trail comes into Carmacks on the broad Yukon River. The Carmacks Community Recreation Centre provides a place for the mushers to get a hot meal and to sleep for a few hours.

Ken Anderson talking with reporters, 2008 race. [Helen Hegener/Northern Light Media]

In his stockinged feet, Lance Mackey visits the checkpoint kitchen, 2008 race [Helen Hegener/Northern Light Media]

Allen Moore arrives at Carmacks on his way to winning the 2013 race. [Scott Chesney/Talespin Media]

Handlers rake and bag the straw after the mushers leave each checkpoint, 2008 race [Helen Hegener/Northern Light Media]

*Left: Lance Mackey enjoys a musher's breakfast at the Braeburn checkpoint, 2008 race. **Above:** Braeburn Lodge, 100 trail miles from Whitehorse. **Below:** Braeburn is justifiably famous for cinnamon buns. [Helen Hegener/Northern Light Media]*

Chapter Eleven ~ Braeburn

World's Largest Cinnamon Buns

Braeburn Lodge, at mile 55 of the Klondike Highway, is one of the last operating original lodges on the route, built soon after the highway opened, around 1952. The checkpoint is known for the tremendous-sized cinnamon buns and generously-proportioned sandwiches which owner Steve Watson prepares. The cinnamon buns are so famous that the nearby Braeburn Airport is also known as Cinnamon Bun Airstrip, although it receives no maintenance and pilots are advised to use caution as there are numerous gopher holes in the 3000' runway.

As the last checkpoint before Whitehorse, Braeburn is often the staging area for more reporters and media camera crews than usual, as the finish line is only 100 trail miles away. Leaving Braeburn it follows the Old Dawson Overland Trail for 70+ miles across lakes and through rolling timbered hills, before dropping onto the frozen Takhini River for approximately 20 miles. That leads to the broad Yukon River for the final ten miles into Whitehorse.

Signs at the Braeburn checkpoint. [Helen Hegener/Northern Light Media]

Teams often run at night when it's cooler for the dogs; Ken Anderson's team, 2008. [Helen Hegener/Northern Light Media]

Mushing along the Takhini River. [Scott Chesney/Talespin Media]

The Takhini River runs into the Yukon River. [Helen Hegener/Northern Light Media]

Above: *Two young Whitehorse fans proudly posed with Lance Mackey the morning after he won the 2008 race, his unprecedented fourth consecutive win. His legendary lead dog Larry, bottom right and page 137, became the only dog in history to win the Golden Harness Award for both the Iditarod and the Yukon Quest. [Helen Hegener/Northern Light Media]*

Chapter Twelve ~ Whitehorse

The Alternate Start and Finish Line

"First a headlamp came into view, then the silhouette of a dog sled, turning the bend off the Yukon River trail and onto the last stretch of the race route. Spectators at the First Avenue finish line of the Yukon Quest then recognized the musher as he came into view.

"'It's Lance!' cried a fan, and cheers erupted across the final race checkpoint in downtown Whitehorse. Lance Mackey became the first musher to win four Yukon Quest sled-dog races in a row at 1:23 this morning."

~from the *Whitehorse Daily Star*, Feb. 20, 2008

As the alternating start and finish line for the Yukon Quest International Sled Dog Race, the Yukon's capital city of Whitehorse has seen many such dramatic moments played out over the years. In 2010 Hans Gatt matched Lance's four wins while also breaking the record for the fastest finish with a time of 9 days and 26 minutes. His time was 23 hours shorter than the previous record, which had been set the year before by Sebastian Schnuelle. In 2012 Tok musher Hugh Neff claimed the championship with Allen Moore of Two Rivers less than one minute behind him. The following year, 2013, Allen Moore reversed the tables and beat Neff in the race to Fairbanks, breaking the record again, and repeating his win and his record-breaking speed on the Fairbanks to Whitehorse route in 2014.

A life-sized husky in a Whitehorse gift shop during the Yukon Quest. [Helen Hegener/Northern Light Media]

Downtown Whitehorse. [Helen Hegener/Northern Light Media]

Downtown Whitehorse. [Helen Hegener/Northern Light Media]

Downtown Whitehorse, the Yukon Quest office is at the end of Main Street. [Helen Hegener/Northern Light Media]

Rob Cooke leaves the Whitehorse chute, 2013 race. [Scott Chesney/Talespin Media]

Four-time champion Lance Mackey leaves Whitehorse, 2013 race. [Scott Chesney/Talespin Media]

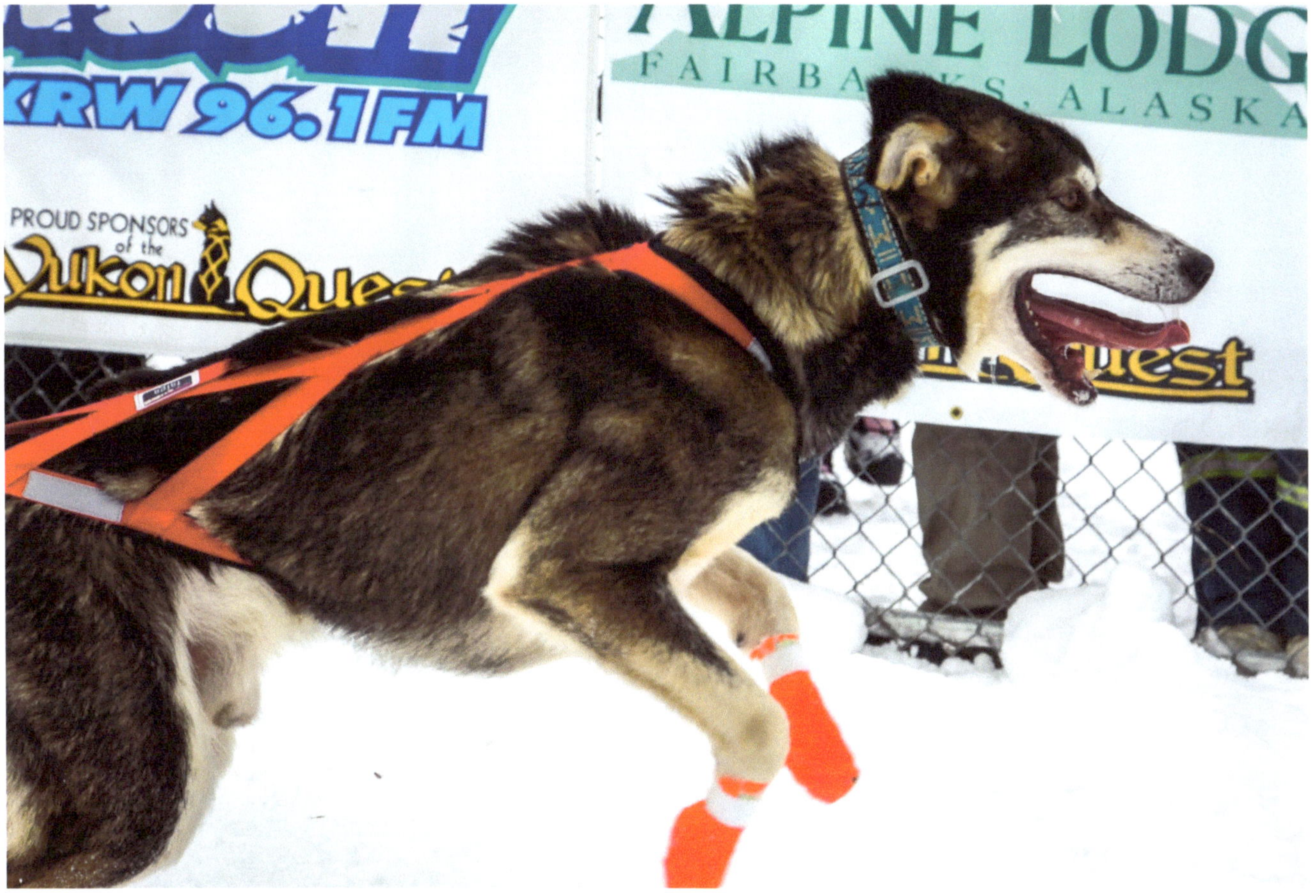

Lance Mackey's leader ready to launch, 2013 race. [Scott Chesney/Talespin Media]

Four-time champion Hans Gatt with his partner Susan Rogan's leaders, 2013 race. [Scott Chesney/Talespin Media]

Brent Sass leaves the Whitehorse chute, 2013 race. [Scott Chesney/Talespin Media]

Veteran Dave Dalton hits the trail in the 2013 race. [Scott Chesney/Talespin Media]

Rookie Susan Rogan leaves Whitehorse, 2013 race. [Scott Chesney/Talespin Media]

Allen Moore bids farewell to his wife, 2000 champion Aliy Zirkle, in the 2013 race. Moore would go on to win this race in record time, and in 2014 he would once again win with a record-breaking pace. [Scott Chesney/Talespin Media]

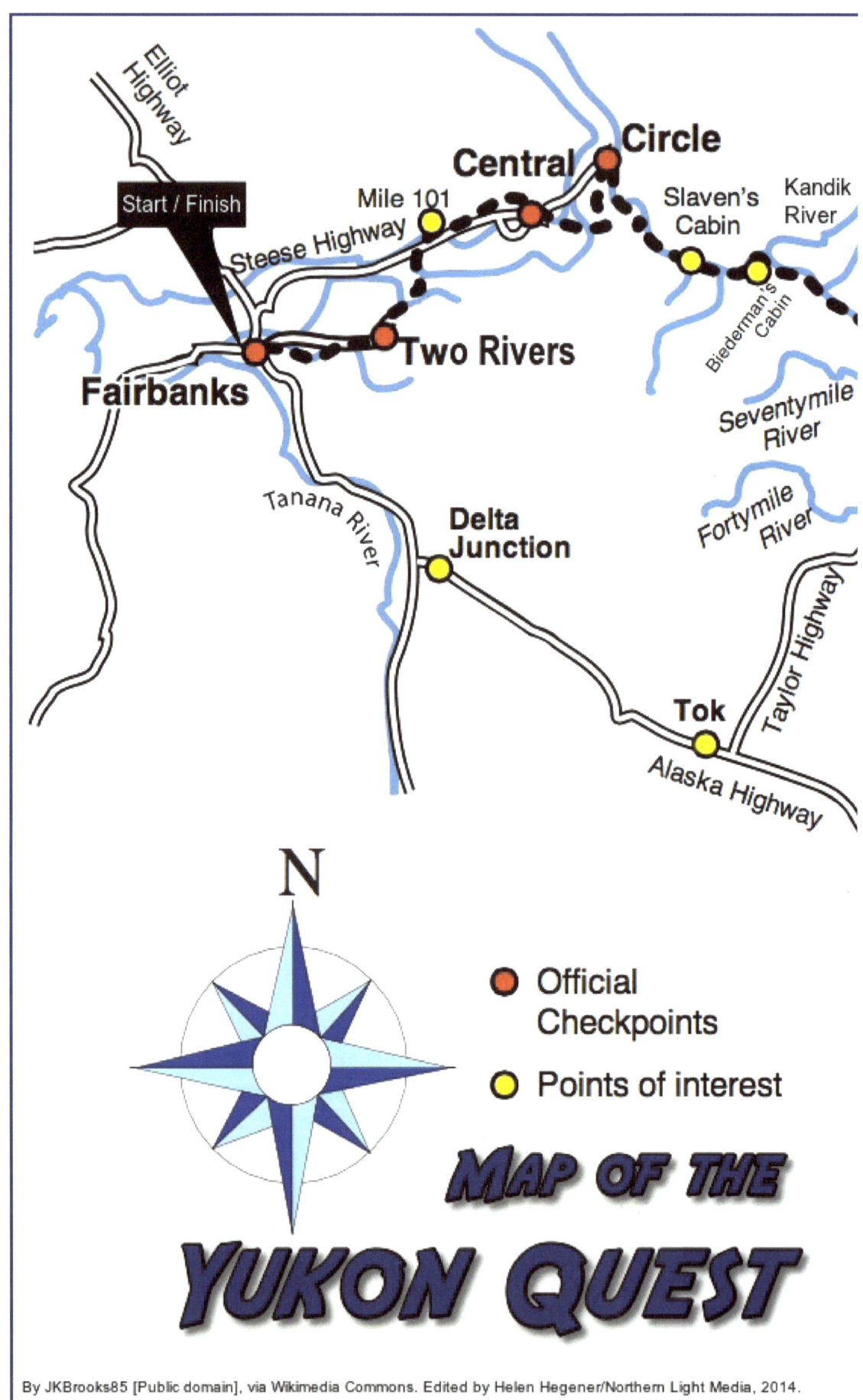

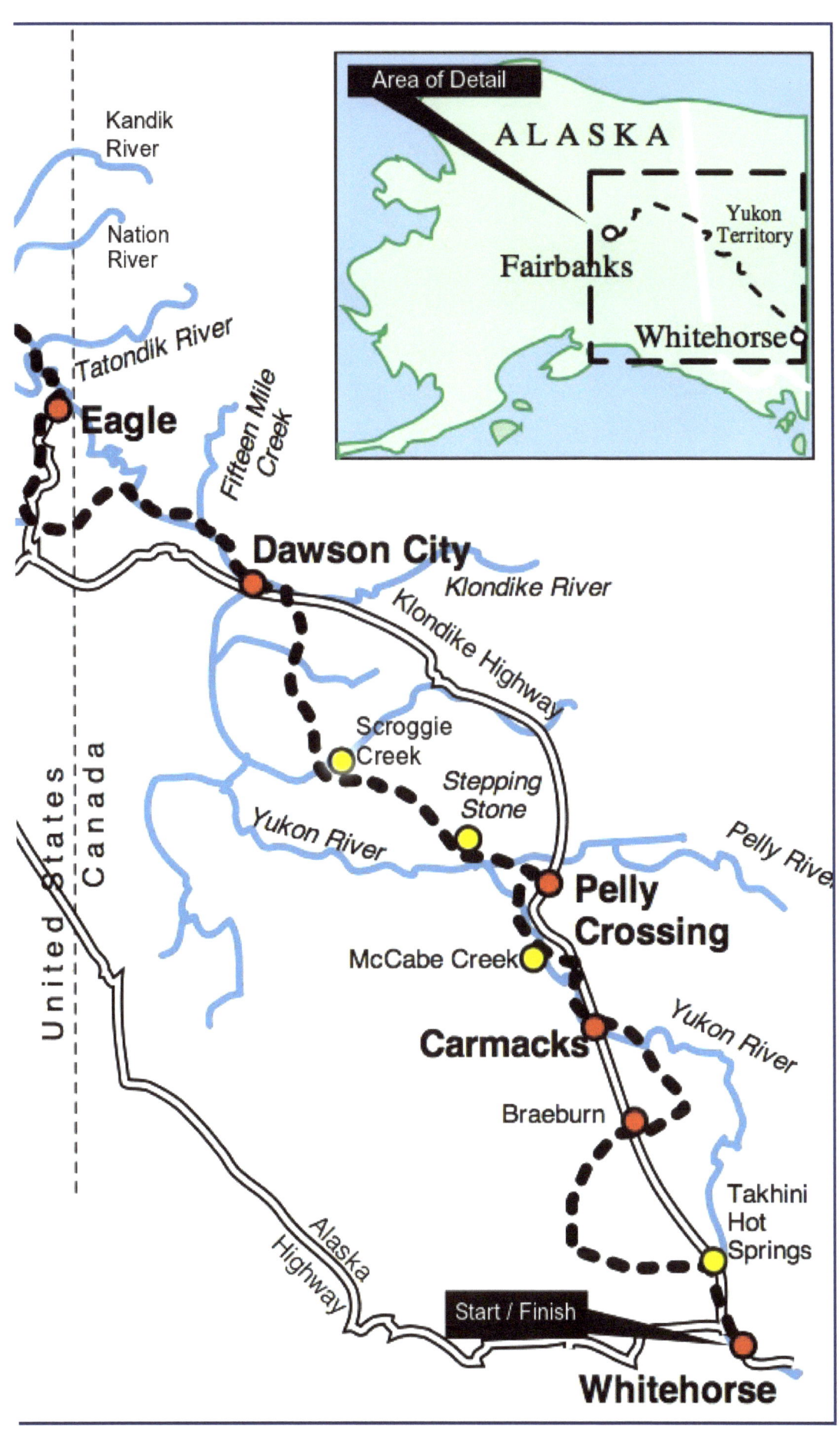

Yukon Quest Books

Racing the White Silence: On the Trail of the Yukon Quest
Adam Killick; Penguin Canada, 2002

Yukon Alone: The World's Toughest Adventure Race
John Balzar; Henry Holt & Co., 1999

Honest Dogs: A Story of Triumph and Regret from the World's Toughest Sled Dog Race
Brian P. O'Donoghue; Epicenter Press, 1999

Yukon Quest: The Story of the World's Toughest Sled Dog Race
Lew Freedman; Epicenter Press, 2010

Yukon Quest Photo Journey
Laurent Dick; Todd Communications, 2003

Yukon Quest: The 1,000 Mile Dog Sled Race through the Yukon and Alaska
John Firth; Lost Moose Press, 1998

Yukon Quest Sled Dog Race
Elizabeth Martin; Arcadia Publishing, 2013

Fulda Yukon Quest: Toughest Race on Earth
Jurgen Hampel and John Firth
Societats Verlag, 1997

Running North: A Yukon Adventure
Ann Mariah Cook; Algonquin Books, 1998

The Lance Mackey Story
Lance Mackey; Zorro Books, 2010

Cold Hands, Warm Heart
Jeff King; Husky Homestead Press, 2008

Long Hard Trails and Sled Dog Tales
Helen Hegener; Northern Light Media, 2014

The Yukon Quest Website
http://www.yukonquest.com

Yukon Quest Champions

1984 - Sonny Lindner
12 days, 0 hours, 5 minutes
1985 - Joe Runyan
11 days, 11 hours, 55 minutes
1986 - Bruce Johnson
14 days, 9 hours, 17 minutes
1987 - Bill Cotter
12 days, 4 hours, 34 minutes
1988 - David Monson
12 days, 5 hours, 6 minutes
1989 - Jeff King
11 days, 20 hours, 51 minutes
1990 - Vern Halter
11 days, 17 hours, 9 minutes
1991 - Charlie Boulding
10 days, 21 hours, 12 minutes
1992 - John Schandelmeier
11 days, 21 hours, 40 minutes
1993 - Charlie Boulding
10 days, 19 hours, 9 minutes
1994 - Lavon Barve
10 days, 22 hours, 44 minutes
1995 - Frank Turner
10 days, 16 hours, 20 minutes
1996 - John Schandelmeier
12 days, 16 hours, 6 minutes
1997 - Rick Mackey
12 days, 5 hours, 55 minutes
1998 - Bruce Lee
11 days, 11 hours, 27 minutes
1999 - Ramy Brooks
11 days, 8 hours, 27 minutes
2000 - Aliy Zirkle
10 days, 22 hours, 57 minutes
2001 - Tim Osmar
11 days, 13 hours, 38 minutes
2002 - Hans Gatt
11 days 4 hours, 22 minutes
2003 - Hans Gatt
10 days 16 hours, 28 minutes
2004 - Hans Gatt
10 days 17 hours, 54 minutes
2005 - Lance Mackey
11 days 32 minutes
2006 - Lance Mackey
10 days, 7 hours, 47 minutes
2007 - Lance Mackey
10 days, 2 hours, 37 minutes
2008 - Lance Mackey
10 days, 12 hours, 14 minutes
2009 - Sebastian Schnuelle
9 days, 23 hours, 20 minutes
2010 - Hans Gatt
9 days, 0 hours, 26 minutes
2011 - Dallas Seavey
10 days, 11 hours, 53 minutes
2012 - Hugh Neff
9 days, 17 hours, 14 minutes
2013 - Allen Moore
8 days, 19 hours, 39 minutes
2014 - Allen Moore
8 days, 14 hours, 21 minutes

Golden Harness Awards

The Champion lead dog(s) receive new golden harnesses and a meal of raw steak at the Finish & Awards Banquet.

1992 - Tess & Arrow
1993 - (Charlie Boulding)
1994 - (Lavon Barve)
1995 - Buck & Grizzly
1996 - Gin Gin
1997 - (Rick Mackey)
1998 - Clovis
1999 - Pretty Boy
2000 - Pedro
2001 - (Tim Osmar)
2002 - Havana & Bonzo
2003 - Havana & Milos
2004 - Havana & Felix
2005 - Hobo Jim & Larry
2006 - Hobo Jim & Larry
2007 - Hobo Jim & Lippy
2008 - Handsome & Rev
2009 - Inuk & Nemo
2010 - Stitch & Kinvig
2011 - Guiness & Diesel
2012 - Walter & Juanita
2013 - Quito
2014 - Quito

Index

Adkins, Darryle, 31, 33
Alaska Highway, 106
Aldrich, Ron, 31, 33
Anderson, Ken, 45, 83, 126, 130, 134
Angelo, Tony, 36
Arctic Circle Hot Springs, 32, 86, 87
Bailey, Jodi, 6, 41, 149
Balzar, John, 13, 118, 121
Barrand, Cindy, 38
Bennett, David, 125, 126
Bergan, Dyan, 2, 32
Berington, Kristy, 40, 74
Berkowitz, Jake, 40, 126
Biederman, Ed, 102, 104
Biederman's Cabin, 102
Braeburn, 19, 20, 132-134
Buser, Martin, 43
Cadzow, Josh, 38
Carmacks, 18, 19, 20, 32, 128-131
Casavant, Normand, 38, 45
Central, 16, 23, 78-85
Chena Hot Springs Road, 16, 24, 36
Chesney, Scott, 7, 74, 75, 109, 114, 115, 118, 120, 126, 127, 129, 131, 135, 140-143
Circle City, 16, 22, 23, 32, 90-99
Circle Hot Springs, 32, 86, 87
Clayton, Murray, 31, 33
Cooke, Rob, 140
Cotter, Bill, 31, 33, 35
Dalton, David, 38, 59, 142
Dawson City, 17, 18, 21, 22, 26, 32, 108-121
Deltour, Sam, 57
DeWolfe, Percy, 104
dog team mail carriers, 102, 104
Downing, Ben, 101, 104
Drobney, Paige, 114

Eagle, 17, 19, 22, 32, 100-105
Eagle Summit, 16, 31, 32, 46, 68, 69, 74-77
Eley, Bob, 31
Ellis, Mike, 53, 55, 78, 80, 83
English, Bob, 31, 32, 33
Ericson, Nick, 31, 33
Ettyne, Nicolay, 41
Failor, Matthew, 59, 60
Fairbanks, 15, 20, 24, 36-51
Fairbanks Daily News-Miner, 68
Firth, John, 35
Foster, Bonnie, 7, 89
Freedman, Lew, 12
Fulda Yukon Quest (Hampel/Firth), 35
Gatt, Hans, 48, 58, 136, 141
Glassburn, Dan, 31, 33
Grilliot, Doug, 36
Halter, Vern, 41
Hayden, Jack, 31, 33
history, 27
Hopkins, Ed, 64, 100
Humphrey, David "Pecos," 31, 33
Huntington, Carl, 35
James, David A., 68
Johnson, Bruce, 31, 33
Kaduce, Dan, 49, 61, 62, 64
Kamper, Peter, 71
Keno, riverboat, 118
Killick, Adam, 31, 46
King, Jeff, 31, 33, 35, 43
Klumb, David, 31, 33
Lindner, Sonny, 31, 33, 35, 39
Lipps, William "Willy," 27
Liss, Shirley, 31, 33
Mackey, Jason, 41
Mackey, Lance, 10, 11, 39, 43, 108, 127, 132, 136, 137, 140, 141
mail carriers, 102, 104
map, 14, 144-145
Martin, Elizabeth "Lizzie," 27, 28, 31, 35
McCowan, Mike, 69
Meet the Mushers, 38-41

Mile 101, 16, 23, 66-73
Mitchell, Lorrina, 28, 31, 33
Moore, Allen, 40, 46, 131, 136, 143
Mushing Magazine, 69
My Yukon Quest Story (Phillips), 69
Neff, Hugh, 39, 40, 44, 129, 136
On Time Delivery (Schneider), 68
Pedersen, Misha, 85, 89
Pelly Crossing, 18, 20, 21, 124-127
Percy DeWolfe Memorial Race, 104
Phillips, Michelle, 69
pink dog, 13
Racing the White Silence (Killick), 31, 46, 101
Ramstead, Karen, 53
Rasmussen House, 92
Riley, Gerald, 31, 33
Robertia, Coleen, 39, 94
Rogan, Susan, 48, 143
Rogers, Jillian, 69
Rosser, Ron, 27
Runyan, Joe, 31, 33, 35
Saari, Matias, 68, 69
Sam, Wilson, 31, 33
Sass, Brent, 39, 56, 98, 142
Schandelmeier, John, 15-24, 25, 96, 102
Schneider, William, S. 68
Schnuelle, Sebastian, 65, 91, 136
Schwing, Emily, 83, 96
Seppala, Leonhard, 43
Service, Robert, 6, 106, 119
Shank, Leroy, 27, 28, 31
Shields, Mary, 28, 31, 33
Slaven, Frank, 102
Slaven's Cabin, 102
Steer, Zack, 39
Stevens, Jack G., 31, 33
Strathe, Cody, 36
Stuck, Hudson, 32, 43
Sutherland, Harry, 31, 33, 35
Sutter, Heidi, 95
Sutton, Iris Wood, 52

Trail Notes for Mushers, 15-24, 102
trail sweeps, 85
Tremblay, Denis, cover, 30
Turnbough, Kevin, 31, 33
Turner, Frank, 31, 33
Two Rivers, 15, 24, 52-65
Two Rivers, John, 31, 33
Ulsom, Joar Leifseth, 41
veterinarians, 116, 117, 127
Wada, Jujiro, 43
Waters, Wendy, 28
West, Abbie, 39, 49, 109
Whaley, Chris, 31, 33
Whitehorse, 15, 20, 136-143
Whitehorse Daily Star, 32
Wickersham, James, 104
Williams, Roger, 27, 28
Williams, Terry, 39
Willomitzer, Gerry, 39
Wilmshurst, Brian, 7, 61, 65
Yuill, Senley, 31, 33,
Yukon Alone (Balzar), 13, 118, 121
Yukon Quest (Freedman), 12,
Yukon Quest (Martin), 27, 28, 31, 35
Yukon Quest 300, 70, 89, 95
Zirkle, Aliy, 47, 142, 147

Uncredited photos:
Pages: 30 (Denis Tremblay), 32 (Dyan Bergan), 146 (left) 147 (left, Aliy Zirkle), 149 (right, Jodi Bailey)
By Eric Vercammen/Northern Light Media

Pages: 8, 9, 12, 13, 26, 27, 29, 146 (right), 147 (right), 148 (both), 149 (left)
By Helen Hegener/Northern Light Media

The Author and the Photographers

Helen Hegener

In 2007 I started down a trail which would lead to a whole new world of adventures when I signed on to travel the Yukon Quest trail as a reporter and videographer. The trail and the people I met along it captivated me, and every February since then has found me traveling the Yukon Quest trail.

I have written numerous books about sled dog racing, the history of mushing, and about the local history of Alaska's Matanuska Valley, which has been my home for many years. In addition to writing about sled dog races I have worked as a volunteer for several, and helped start two: the Northern Lights 300 and the Holy Grail of Mushing, the Iditarod.

I've enjoyed being a recreational musher in the past, and I still own two dogsleds, but I only have one old husky now, and he greatly dislikes being hitched to a sled.

Eric Vercammen

Avid fans of sled dog racing can be found worldwide, but one would be hard pressed to find a more enthusiastic proponent of the sport than my friend Eric.

For several years he has made the trip from his home in Antwerp, Belgium to Anchorage, Alaska, to follow the Iditarod Trail Sled Dog Race, and he has traveled all the way to the end of the trail in Nome as a fan and a photographer. Over the years many of his striking photographs have appeared with my articles about the Iditarod and other races for the online news magazine, *Alaska Dispatch*.

In 2013, after years of listening to my stories about the Yukon Quest, Eric took a break from the Iditarod and traveled the Yukon Quest trail with me and our friend Albert Marquez, another fine photographer and race enthusiast, and - like us - a pizza lover!

Scott Chesney

I have admired and appreciated my friend Scott's dynamically beautiful photographs of the Yukon Quest mushers and dogs for many years, as he is a professional race photographer of the first caliber.

Scott has worked as part of an independent media team tracking the race, producing inspiring and engaging photographs which portrayed the essence of the hardworking mushers and dogs, and captured the spirit and the excitement of being on the trail.

I've spent time alongside him in the start and finish chute, on the trail, and at checkpoints, always trying to capture the action and the story-pictures, but never even coming close to achieving what he does with a camera. And so, when he offered his beautiful photographs for this book, I was, needless to say, overjoyed.

Also from Northern Light Media

http://northernlightmedia.wordpress.com

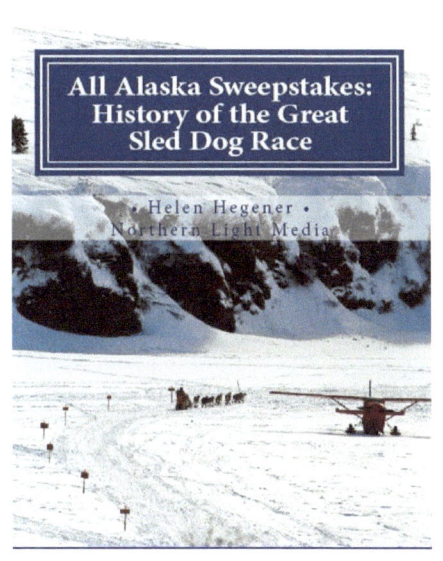

Along Alaskan Trails

A collection of true stories about Alaskan sled dogs and the role they played in the development of the north, with dozens of historic photos from the archives of the Alaska State Library, the University of Alaska Fairbanks, and other sources.

In every part of this great land, from southeastern Alaska to the farthest northern tip of the continent, sled dogs were the most dependable and often the only form of transportation. This book tells the stories of intrepid mushers such as Leonhard Seppala, Scotty Allan, Slim Williams, Jujiro Wada and others.

Along Alaskan Trails, Adventures in Sled Dog History, by Helen Hegener. Published in July, 2012. 90 pages, 160 b/w photos, 8.5" x 11" format.

The All Alaska Sweepstakes

With colorful drivers like "Scotty" Allan and Leonhard Seppala, who each won the race three times, the All Alaska Sweepstakes was an eagerly anticipated annual event. In 1983 the Nome Kennel Club sponsored the 75th Anniversary race, and Rick Swenson took home the $25,000.00 purse.

Then, in 2008, for the 100th Anniversary of the event, the Nome Kennel Club offered the richest purse ever for a sled dog race: $100,000.00 winner-take-all, and mushers from all across the state signed on for the historic race to Candle and back.

The All Alaska Sweepstakes, by Helen Hegener, photos by Jan DeNapoli, Joe May, Donna Quante and others. Published in 2013. 160 pages, over 350 full color photos. 8.5" x 11" format.

Appetite & Attitude

Lance Mackey is the world's preeminent long distance sled dog racer. He made racing history when he won two 1,000 mile races back-to-back, the Yukon Quest and the Iditarod, with most of the same dogs – an incredible feat of endurance, long considered almost impossible, which changed how mushers think about what their dogs are capable of achieving.

Lance then went on to win both races a total of four times each, including an unprecedented four straight Iditarod wins. He is one of the greatest mushers who ever lived. In this 45-minute high definition video Lance talks about his races, his dogs, and the roots of his mushing history.

Appetite and Attitude. 45 minute HD-DVD.

www.ingramcontent.com/pod-product-compliance
Lightning Source LLC
Chambersburg PA
CBHW041524220426
43670CB00002B/27